The DNA of Collaboration

Unlocking the Potential of
21st Century Teams

Chris Jones

@sourcepov

Published by Amberwood Media Group
PO Box 31726 | Charlotte, NC 28231

**The DNA of Collaboration: Unlocking the Potential
of 21st Century Teams**

ISBN 978-0-9787566-1-1

Also available as an E-Book on Amazon Kindle
More information and updates at http://collaborationdna.com

Cover design and photo by Amberwood Media Group
Cover photo: Umstead Park, Raleigh, NC

to

NIKKI, COREY & PAIGE

my three constant sources of
inspiration

Table of Contents

Acknowledgements

No surprise that a book about collaboration has been a product of collaboration from the outset. Many of the ideas in these pages were first voiced by others. For their collective input and inspiration, I owe a huge debt of gratitude.

In a nutshell, this book is about how ideas move through organizations. It's a broad frame that's required considerable reflection and research—over a number of years—to piece together the contributing factors.

A handful of thinkers have shaped my perspectives so profoundly that I want to give them special mention right up front. In the broad study of how we perceive and describe problems, Thomas Kuhn's *Structure of Scientific Revolutions* (1962) is one of the most influential books on my fairly full shelf. His notion of paradigms and the dynamics of paradigm change established critical bedrock for this journey. Peter Senge in *The Fifth Discipline* (1990) also laid important groundwork. He advanced key concepts in organizational learning like *systems thinking* and *mental models* that gave Kuhn's broader frame a more personal dimension. And in terms of the organizational landscape, no one paints it with more breathtaking or provocative strokes than Margaret Wheatley; in *A Simpler Way* (1996) she challenges each of us— relentlessly—to rethink our organizations and our place in them. Each of these authors has been a catalyst for me, creating key inflection points. Reading their words when I did changed the trajectory of my thinking.

Over the course of my career, two authors and their watershed books helped advance my grasp of organizational behavior: Rosabeth Moss Kanter in *The Change Masters* (1980), and Daniel Goleman in *Primal Leadership* (2002). In fundamental and important ways, they both helped me understand why people and teams do what they do. To this day, their ideas are deeply infused in my thoughts on leadership and group dynamics. More recently, through research for this book, my views of collaboration's possibilities have expanded upon that foundation, enriched through the equally important work of Chris Argyris, Carol Dweck, Glenda Eoyang, John Hagel, Charles Handy, Andrew McAfee, Beth Noveck, Daniel Pink, Thomas Stewart and Don Tapscott. It's an influential group, offering us a host of influential ideas. Their many and diverse contributions are reflected in the pages ahead.

I can call out several individuals who first connected me with key concepts and sources for my research; many thanks to Diane Court, Christian DeNeef, Angela Dunn, Corey Jones, Julian Loren, Mary Nations, Eric Threatt and Bruce Watluck. I've come to appreciate the value of a trusted network that's comprised of deep thinkers; their contributions to this undertaking—however indirect they may have seemed at the time—have made the case many times over. It's worth noting all except two of the connectors listed here were contacts initiated via social networks.

My review team has shouldered huge burdens during this project. They've made *The DNA of Collaboration* fundamentally better in so many ways that I'm at a loss to quantify the impact. They helped to shape it, focus it, and make it more accessible. Suffice it to say that I can't thank them enough. My deep gratitude to friends and colleagues Christine Egger, Renee Hopkins, Alasdair Munn, Jenna Ream, Jennifer Sertl, Paula Thornton and Kim Walters.

First-time authors have a special but somewhat complicated relationship with their editors. I've told mine, Meredith Gould, that throughout this project she's helped to make the impossible seem possible. She was tough and direct when she needed to be, wielding her editorial axe gently—and sometimes not so gently—as the situation required, but she remained supportive at every step. I have learned much about writing from her, and I look forward to learning more.

No one supported me more in the critical early stages of this project than my dear friend Janet Bolton-Fontenot. She listened to my ramblings when the notion of a book was still vague and elusive. She only rarely admitted to growing weary—though I knew otherwise—and I can't thank her enough for her tireless support and encouragement.

I'd be remiss not to mention those in my global social networks who have been a part of this journey. Over the last several years, these individuals have shared their insights and responded to mine, challenging my thinking, and raising the bar on what's possible in virtual collaboration. With the obvious risk that I'll leave someone out, I offer my enthusiastic appreciation to Mary Abraham, Eric Andersen, Jamie Billingham, Meghan Biro, Jane Bozarth, Mike Brown, LeAnna Carey, Hutch Carpenter, Steve Cassady, Marion Chapsal, Amber Cleveland, Marsha Collier, Mack Collier, Marcia Conner, Caroline Di Diego, Becky Ellis, Paul Ellis, Amanda Fenton, Bill Free, Mark Gammon, Stan Garfield, Nahum Gershon, Sean Grainger, Jacob Greenwood, Nikki Groom, Breanne Harris, June Holley, David Holzmer, Ken Homer, Cathryn Hrudicka, Carsten Hucho, Gwen Ishmael, Michael Josefiwicz, Saul Kaplan, Brian Kenney, Joe Kikta, Charee Klimek, John Kosic, Valdis Krebs, Diana Laufenburg, Julian Loren, Drew Marshall, Gregg Masters, Elizabeth McCaffrey, Brandie McCallum, Jeff Merrell, Christopher Meaton, Betsey Merkel, Andrea Meyer, Sharon Mostyn, Venessa Miemis, Greg Miller, Bernd Nurnberger, Cameron Norman, Jeffrey Phillips, Rachel Pickett, Boris

Pluskowski, Clark Quinn, Mary Ann Reilly, Bas Reus, Joseph Ruiz, Joe Sanchez, Kelli Schmith, Paul Schuk, Kim Sherrell, Alex Shipee, Rabia Shirazi, Jay Smethurst, Marc Sniukas, Luis Suarez, Robert Swanwick, Autom Tagsa, Kendall Thiessen, David Timony, Andrew Townley, John Tropea, Mandy Vavrinak and Elizabeth Weiland. I can recall numerous and insightful conversations with everyone on this list. I'm confident that I'm richer—and far better informed—for having had the privilege of getting to know them.

A special thanks on the home stretch to my proof reader, Emily Clark, and to team of supporters who magically emerged in the final weeks of the project when the support was needed most: Claire Crossley, Alicia Durand, Shannon Fatigante, Cameron Jones, Karen Jones, Tascha Kiesser, Cat Levine, Dawn Lilley, Ashley Perez and Michele Martin.

And finally, my deep gratitude to the up-and-coming Nashville band *Pines of Porter*, for their insights on collaboration in action.

In various ways all of these people are collaborators, whether as mentors, trusted advisors, connectors or catalysts. Some are family. Many have become friends. I'm privileged to have served as your understudy, note-taker and curator, as we begin to frame the exciting opportunities that intentional collaboration affords.

I hope what follows proves thoughtful, doing justice to what we've shared and learned together.

I also hope that, in the end, I'm getting some of this right.

A Note to Readers

While *The DNA of Collaboration* can be read front to back, you may want to focus on the content that aligns with collaboration challenges currently at hand. Don't hesitate to dive into the middle. Some readers have reported getting value by using certain sections of the book in isolation, especially where groups are already working well in some areas.

If you're focusing on these work groups:	These collaboration insights may be most valuable:	In these PARTs of the book:					
		PROLOGUE	1 FRAMEWORKS	2 MESSAGING	3 RELATIONSHIPS	4 FLOW	5 POSSIBILITIES
▪ Corporate employees ▪ Project managers ▪ Knowledge workers	Learning how to better solve problems in teams	●	●	●	●	●	
▪ Executives	Organizational dynamics & ways to drive change	●		●	●		●
▪ Small businesses ▪ Non-profits ▪ Community leaders	Getting people working together	●			●	●	
▪ Change agents ▪ HR/OD specialists ▪ KM practitioners	Achieving the learning organization	●	●	●	●	●	●
▪ CIOs ▪ IT teams ▪ Consultants	Planning and deployment of collaboration processes & tools	●	●			●	●

The discussion on these topics is continuing online. Visit the book's website at http://collaborationdna.com for updates.

Prologue

My morning's hike had been vigorous. The North Carolina autumn was well past its peak, the afternoon chill already upon me. Approaching a favorite vantage point, I could hear the sound of the mountain stream as it tumbled down a fall in the rocks. I crested the ridge above the falls to survey the scene. I tarried a moment, perhaps two. But it wasn't until I'd turned for home that my eye fell upon objects in motion: two leaves, dancing, chasing each other helter-skelter in the current below the falls. They raced forward, impatient and determined, anxious to get where they were going. And then suddenly, abruptly, their progress stalled. The leaves drifted now in lazy circles, almost touching, hesitating. It lasted just a moment, maybe the span of a breath. Then, like a shot, they leapt back into the current to resume the race, tumbling once more, dancing, until both leaves were gone from my view, never to be seen again.

The flow of insights in our daily lives is very much the same.[1] Our thoughts surge past us, often before we notice them. Like leaves on a fast-moving stream, ideas dart in and out of view. Some might get trapped in an eddy, or become stranded by some offending obstruction. But in special cases—the ones we'll explore—specific ideas can be pulled from the flow for study.

Odds are against it, of course: the thought-stream of life is fast and furious. Invariably, we're distracted by the priorities of the moment. That's all the more reason to stop and reflect, putting ourselves in the metaphor. *We must reach into the water and take a leaf from the stream.*

The ability to take hold of our fleeting ideas, to study them, exchange them, and consider them deeply is what separates effective collaborators from the rest. Our ability to learn from each other depends largely on our ability to connect in real-time, to focus, and to communicate our ideas fully and clearly. We need to find new ways to make our best ideas matter. Too often we fail to engage, and our ideas race away quickly, out of reach.

Collaboration can generate a torrent of insights and it can be hard to get our bearings. And when we dare to enter the stream, we face difficult choices. Do we paddle against the current in pursuit of our own ideas? Do we cross to the opposite bank for a different perspective? Do we grab hold of a branch or rock to hold our position? Or do we set down our paddle and go with the flow, letting the current carry us where it may? Most will choose the latter option. To paddle against the current—or frankly, in any direction—is to consume precious effort. In the 21st century, the stakes of survival seem ever higher. We've become tactical in our thinking, cynical, at times even defensive.[2] Afraid that poor decisions create risk, we avoid decisions and the deep thinking they require whenever possible. It's far easier to drift with the mainstream, content that we're moving, consoled that virtually everyone else is going in the same direction.

It's time to chart a new course.

Navigating in the waters of intention and discovery is a profound challenge for the 21st Century and most have failed to see it. More and more, learning and creativity are left behind, as we relegate initiative, teamwork, and the hard work of problem solving to others. We find ourselves operating below our full potential, at a loss to explain why.

In *The DNA of Collaboration* we'll explore all of these challenges. We'll learn what it takes to navigate the fast-moving stream of insights that collaboration demands. We'll look at barriers that limit our chances and constrain our choices. We'll also look at enablers, ways we can open up to new insights and expand our collaborative opportunities.

Organization dynamics are complex and difficult to predict, and the powerful undercurrents can be difficult to see. We must ask:

- **Can we distill the patterns that guide our behaviors?**
- **What does it take in the 21st Century to spark action, initiative and engagement?**
- **What is the ongoing impact of organizational silos, where separate departments compete for limited resources at the expense of the whole?**
- **Why can't people in teams just get along?**

These are important and significant questions. Our inability to work together places a huge burden on an organization's ability to solve problems, the fundamental task at the core of everything we do. Challenges impact our productivity, constraining our ability to improve our business processes and blocking our grander aspirations for strategic organizational change and marketplace innovation.

In the 1980's and 90's, Rosabeth Moss Kanter, Chris Argyris, Peter Senge, and Margaret Wheatley began writing in great depth about the untapped potential of people working together more effectively. They built a compelling vision of what a *learning organization* might accomplish. But in the decades since, meaningful progress has failed to materialize.[3]

In *The DNA of Collaboration* I've started to sketch out a path forward. Across a broad terrain of organizational settings—places where people come together to try to solve problems—I've seen the same patterns of dysfunctional behavior played out again and again. I've seen inertia, frustration and bureaucratic malaise, perpetuated by smart people that ought to have known better—many of them hoping, however naively, that "this time it would be different." In bureaucracies the world over, our only consensus may be our shared sense of complacency.

It's a maddening question, really.

What's wrong with the modern organization?

My first encounter with organizational gridlock happened early in my career, just a few years out of college. Clutching my copy of Kanter's classic *Change Masters*, I devoured her every word. It seemed, even then, perhaps in the naiveté of my youth, there had to be a way of doing work that was better than organizational bureaucracy, a place where ideas could flow across boundaries in useful ways.[4]

I've experienced several rewarding collaborative interludes in the years since I first read *Change Masters*. I've seen collaboration work and I know it's possible. I've been on teams where ideas flowed seamlessly to places they needed to flow, where debates transformed almost effortlessly into consensus, where complex projects and hard decisions were always tackled with energy, professional skill, and a positive attitude. It's not that people can't collaborate. Something has been holding them back.

I wrote this book in response to a set of deep frustrations—my own, and those of others—which are routinely centered in the areas of poor team productivity, stranded ideas and a raft of dysfunctional behaviors. Our ability to make useful progress in organizations is constrained, if not in total gridlock. I've heard a persistent outcry for change that to me seems increasingly urgent. So in late 2009 I set out on a journey of discovery, in hopes I could learn more about what might be causing these problems. The more I learned, the more I wanted to know. In the months that followed, as the puzzle pieces began to take shape, I resolved to share what I'd learned. I wanted to give back in some measure to those who'd shared so much with me. At the core of intentional collaboration is a kindred spirit, a quest to discover possibilities together. To me, that's a powerful formula for personal and organizational growth. It's the same energy that motivated my thinking and guided my research, shaping the ideas in the pages ahead.

Beyond the organization and in the spaces between them, I believe collaboration is the only viable path to social change on the global scale. Again, traditional paths have reached gridlock. But by working together, we gain incredibly profound insights about ourselves and our potential, and to literally redefine what is possible. Margaret Wheatley said it well:

> *Relationships change us, reveal us, and evoke more from us ... only when we join with others do our gifts become visible, even to ourselves.*[5]

I've found intention to be a powerful force of our human nature, yet we so easily lose touch with it. We settle for drift and follow the whims of the current, with no particular destination in mind.

Collaborating with intention can help us break the cycle. Through interaction with like-minded colleagues, we can bring purpose and meaning back into focus. When we look up from our collaborative work, we sometimes find ourselves on a new and exciting path.

We might even find we're starting to make a difference.

Those who seek to collaborate wear many hats. They are business managers, executives, community leaders, school teachers, neighbors, and public servants. They're knowledge workers of all varieties.[6] Many of them are change agents, holding on to the promise of new and better solutions, only to find themselves perpetually working against the grain[7] and investing herculean efforts to move their ideas forward, yearning for a method to the madness, hoping to foster conditions for deeper, more expansive creative thinking in teams.[8]

I've discussed these challenges in open public forums for the last three years and I've learned a great deal.[9] With the expansion of social media—the technology that enables open exchange of content and ideas—public conversations have begun to emerge out of nowhere, fueled by dialog among colleagues, acquaintances and even strangers. The Internet provides the communication vehicle. Tools like Twitter and blogging sites like WordPress provide a space for the exchange of ideas.

Suddenly, collaboration is showing up in new places.

Virtual collaboration may not be for everyone. But for me, these conversations have opened up an incredibly unique perspective on the levels of collaboration that are possible.[10] They've also prompted me to ask several additional questions:

- **Why can strangers collaborate in open spaces, while motivated, highly incented commercial teams routinely fail?**
- **What factors are different across these collaboration scenarios?**
- **What is it about large organizations that cause collaborators to have to work against the grain?**

These questions have fueled my thinking. We'll unpack them in the pages ahead. We'll explore the extent to which barriers to collaboration lie within us as individuals. We'll explore culture as a crucial driver of behavior. And we'll look at risk-taking. It's okay to be wrong in this brave new world of learning and discovery but for some this may prove profoundly difficult.[11]

If navigating the flow of basic insights is a challenge, dealing with abstract ideas and the shifting of context is like running the rapids. How we contemplate and describe knowledge can prove difficult, yet doing so is foundational to how we learn. From Aristotle to Newton, from Socrates and Plato to Descartes, from Kant to Kuhn and Polanyi, the competing frameworks for how we describe knowledge have been debated for centuries. It's a fascinating discussion[12] but in *The DNA of Collaboration* we will avoid most of those debates so that we can remain grounded and practical. I'll touch on a few historical inflection points and relevant theories in the Notes, but collaboration's many challenges require us to stay focused. Can we get better at solving problems in teams? Is it possible to get better at learning how to learn? I answer *yes* on both counts; collaboration will be our common entry point.

Only in recent years has the emergence of new thinking begun to reveal what's required, and a quick glance at the news makes the point. Major issues facing world leaders require a joint, cross-disciplinary—and yes, collaborative—approach due to geopolitical fissures that date back several millennia and serve to divide us all.[13] We live in a world where specialists can no longer go it alone, a world where selfish notions like "I got there first" reflect ego, control, and power in unhealthy proportions. For all of our progress and improvements in quality of life, we have acquired cultural biases that are proving to be counter-productive over the long run.

My training in engineering and computer science tells me to take all those difficult problems apart and break them into smaller, solvable pieces. But my modern instincts, now infused with *complexity thinking*, tell me the opposite, with a bias for leaving sub-component structures alone and letting our insights about them flow where they may. I'm increasingly convinced it's not about picking one paradigm over the other,[14] the approach usually advocated by experts. Increasingly, it's clear that a middle ground is needed.

Diverse approaches, like diverse people, can work together.

The industrialized West is consumed by cause-and-effect thinking, a powerful force baked into our empirical science-based education. It feeds our deep obsession for data. But there are other, equally compelling ways of looking at knowledge that are based on rational thinking, centuries-old knowledge frameworks[15] and a new understanding of complexity. Opening our minds to new mental models requires that we respect and appreciate paradigms that are not our own. A shift from personal or discipline-centric models to cross-functional or team-embraced versions can be a profound one for many. Making this leap lies on the critical path for collaborative success. We must begin to realize that alternate conceptual frames are viable, and that the most valuable frames may not be our own.

The challenge ahead can seem daunting. Each of us holds significant potential in our thoughts and ideas about the world. But that potential is often constrained, held back by a personal decision that links directly to our willingness to approach others for help.

Collaboration is a choice.

If we're to achieve change in the world, or to seek it closer to home, across our organizations and within our teams, we must take confident steps forward—with intention—to embrace the many challenges that true collaboration requires. The call for action is clear, as the stakes mount ever higher.

The stream of ideas is a value stream. Much work lies ahead to learn to navigate it, and the current is strong. We'd best get started.

Chris Jones
Charlotte, NC
December 2011

PART 1: FRAMING OUR POTENTIAL

"A company in the information age is really a beehive of ideas, impacting how they should be setup and run, and how they should compete."

Thomas Stewart

1 – Introduction

Where to Begin?

Let's start with a very basic definition of collaboration.

I describe it as *"solving problems in teams."*

It sounds straightforward, but I've found it's much more difficult in practice than it seems in principle. What's hard for one person to figure out can be even harder when more thinkers are added. Insights surge around us, a convoluted flow of inputs and outputs that vie for our attention. Hearing different voices in support of competing insights can prove chaotic and hard to follow. Consensus can be difficult to achieve, making common ground elusive.

Look around. What environment is most significant in your world? Is it a commercial one, like a corporation or small business? Is it a social institution like a public school, a local community, or a nonprofit? Is it a church, a synagogue, or a mosque? Is it a governmental venue, like town council chambers, or an office in the state or provincial capital? Or perhaps you face team-based projects closer to home, working in small groups among family and friends. Success in any of these arenas requires people skills and social skills, and the ability to influence others.

Yet collaboration can fail in all of these places.

Large organizations provide plenty of scenarios to reinforce this point. Here are just a few of them:

Situations Where Collaboration Can Matter Most	Typical Problems Observed (Current State)	Frameworks	Messaging	Relationships	Flow	Possibilities
Team Building across Boundaries. Mergers or acquisitions result in local operations that work independently, unable to tap/create broader synergies. Can apply to alliances.	Confusion on Roles Unclear Accountabilities Lack of cooperation	●	●	●		●
Cross-Functional Design Projects. A company needs to bring a new product to market, but department experts have trouble working together.	Inability to communicate Lack of cooperation	●	●	●	●	●
Strategy Change & Realignment. To improve its market position, a company wants to redefine itself and its business model, but few have a clear picture of what that means.	Confusion Concerns & insecurity Lack of cooperation	●	●	●	●	●
Process De-Calcification. Years of "business as usual" have created significant inefficiency in how things work but the organization is too comfortable with the status quo.	Apathy Resistance to change Lack of cooperation	●	●			
Customer Service. Unusual customer requirements can cause service teams to scramble, forcing them to work creatively across internal boundaries to solve a problem.	Unclear Accountabilities Lack of cooperation	●	●	●		●
Organization Change. New leadership structures can be unsettling at first, requiring employees to keep an open mind about the future.	Resistance to change Lack of cooperation	●	●	●		●

FIGURE 1 – Problems where Collaboration is Useful
Situations in organizations where a focus on team-based problem-solving can help

Collaboration can be hard work. Many wonder if it's even worth it. I believe collaboration is *more* than worth it. We just need to understand it better, and to get better at doing it.

Here's how we'll attack it in *The DNA of Collaboration.*

Framing Our Potential (Pt.1): It's important that we lay a solid foundation for our study of collaboration; we'll discuss the many challenges we face when we seek to solve problems in teams. Included will be:

- Practical collaboration scenarios, to get us thinking
- Four Power Tools that help us navigate difficult problems, including abstraction, context, root cause analysis, and the development of conceptual frameworks
- Outcomes, a description of what collaborators can produce; we'll look at raw insights, and how those can evolve in different contexts to become ideas, solution models and actual solutions

Messaging (Pt.2): Improving our communication skills is critically important, so we'll explore:

- Intention, including our commitments and motivations
- The power of words, and our ability to manage their semantic nuances
- The rich variety that metaphor brings to our discussion, with its subtle ability to help us understand abstract concepts
- Storytelling itself, weaving all of these elements together to connect our listeners with deeper meaning

Relationships (Pt.3): Exploring the dynamics of meaningful engagement is one of the strongest determinants of success in collaboration, so we'll take a look at:

- Active listening
- What happens when our logic is hijacked by mental shortcuts ("heuristics"), instinctive reactions, or visceral emotions like fear
- The challenges imposed by organizational culture
- The challenges of contrarians, facing the formidable forces of ego, power and control.
- Elements of the trusting organization

Flow (Pt.4): Moving from a structured approach to one that's more dynamic requires a significant change in how we think and how we approach team interaction; we'll investigate:

- Productive and flexible work spaces, including both traditional and virtual modes of interaction
- Definition of key roles
- Understanding of complex team dynamics, and the many aspects of this that can impact success, including affinity, diversification and adaptive governance
- Processes that can adapt to needs at different scales
- Balanced objectives, to navigate opposing forces

Possibilities (Pt.5): Imagining the future of learning and knowledge sharing, as new capabilities emerge before us:

- Measuring our new skills and potential
- Transforming knowledge management, allowing people to share insights across increasingly connected organizations
- Understanding and ultimately mastering the core demands of critical thinking
- Harnessing the fascinating implications of our emerging collaboration lexicon, based on concepts of complexity

The study of organizational dynamics has a long history, offering several interesting vantage points. Many academic disciplines (or *domains*) have a stake in what it means to collaborate effectively. FIGURE 2 on the next page provides a summary. These practitioners and their perspectives can help us to both define and refine the elements of *The DNA of Collaboration* and I'll continue to cite them as we go, highlighting their input. Many thinkers in these disciplines have spent decades researching the topic of team dynamics, and we'll need their help.

Of course it's not as easy as adding up all their ideas and circulating a list. Trying to gain consensus among highly diverse groups—with a multitude of domain experts at the table—is difficult. In fact, it is one of our central challenges. Gaining agreement on the approach for collaboration can be as difficult as collaboration itself. It's like herding cats: no sooner do you get a few to agree to stay in the box than another two or three jump back out. We need a unifying objective. So let's add the element of purpose to our definition:

> **Intentional collaboration is "solving problems in teams, with a designed, thoughtful approach and a specific outcome in mind."**

With this broader definition, it's easier to see how quickly we can raise the bar beyond the limits of casual brainstorming.

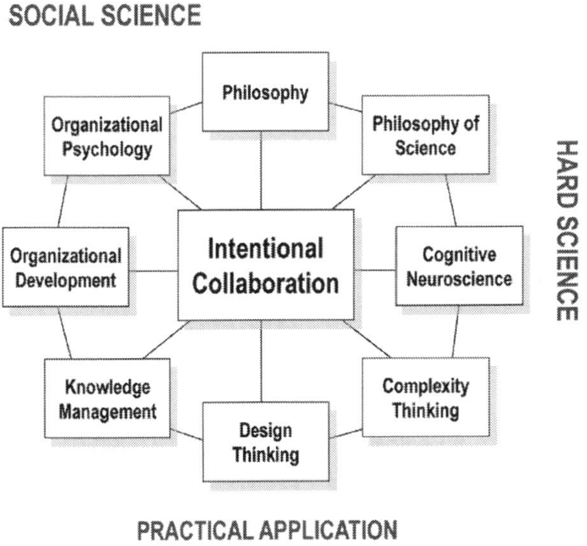

SOCIAL SCIENCE

Philosophy

Organizational Psychology

Philosophy of Science

HARD SCIENCE

Organizational Development

Intentional Collaboration

Cognitive Neuroscience

Knowledge Management

Design Thinking

Complexity Thinking

PRACTICAL APPLICATION

FIGURE 2 – Collaboration Experts
Eight disciplines that heavily influence how we approach
intentional collaboration

With a subtle shift to *intention* we find we're onto something more. Adding the element of rigor, our approach suddenly presumes a desire to achieve something, to invest effort that will lead to a useful result. It's harder because we have to think about what we're doing. But by adding intention we demand more focus, significantly increasing our potential to produce a valuable set of outcomes.

FIGURE 2 illustrates that problem-solving in teams requires a set of integrated activities with many dimensions, each contributing to the end result: an organizational *capability* that was not present before.[16] It really comes down to reaping what you sow; with focus and intention, something incredibly useful can emerge: new possibilities.[17]

How Ambitious Can We Be?

Our Western society tends to dramatize innovation as "aha" moments or laboratory breakthroughs by famous inventors, but many (if not most) of the innovative scientific achievements of the last century were fueled by on-going dialogue. The search for scientific knowledge is often compared to solving a puzzle. Quantum mechanics is a notable example, where conversations among Einstein, Bohr, Pauli, and Heisenberg produced significant new thinking that, over many years, led to ultimate breakthroughs.[18]

In a Hollywood-infused culture that idolizes larger-than-life moments, we imagine a block buster movie script when the reality is more mundane: people coming together to share ideas. Small wonder we're quick to discount collaboration when it sparks organically (*"we were just kicking some ideas around"*) but then get frustrated when we can't reproduce similar results on demand. We over-simplify, then grow impatient. We search for silver bullets, and complain when none can be found.

What is the scale of challenges we seek to take on? Is there a limit to the kinds of problems that *The DNA of Collaboration* can address? Let's look at a few examples.

Example 1: Business Strategy. Let's start with a business problem that appears in FIGURE 1, a strategic change that may warrant development of a new business model. In his recent book *Business Model Innovation Factory* (2012), Saul Kaplan expands fully on this example, pointing out the challenges that come with defining how a company produces value for its customers. He points to a variety of well-known examples, including Wal-Mart's "always low prices" and BMW's "ultimate driving machine." These are both reinforced in the minds of consumers via advertising, but these two companies have invested deeply over many decades to master relatively unique business models that seek to make their stated objectives credible to consumers, supported by their actual experience.

For many other companies, Kaplan points out how gaps in *systems thinking* and a general disdain for abstract ideas like business models can keep many organizations from contemplating unique value propositions like the two mentioned here, let alone charting a course for achieving them.[19] It's an important example. Concepts as basic as how a company makes money or why it has (or doesn't have) a competitive edge can escape the agenda of senior management, or become mired in the faulty mental models of a select few executives who own the strategy. Kaplan notes that business queries about the "why" and "how" of strategy often send executives looking for their organizational charts, again demonstrating a reliance on hierarchy to explain how things work, not an understanding of the business (as a system) itself.

Organizations can break through these hurdles with focus and rigor, if there is a recognition that understanding the flow of value as a framework or business model is fundamental to the company's success in the marketplace.

It's not a question of every executive learning to wield Michael Porter's "Five Forces" at the whiteboard,[20] but there must be recognition that somewhere in the organization such knowledge will be planted, nourished, and ultimately evangelized throughout the organization. Longer-term, a deep understanding of how an organization delivers value needs to become part of the culture, with its core themes surfacing routinely in everyday language. These are the kinds of business problems that the application of *The DNA of Collaboration* can address.

Now let's look now at social systems more broadly, areas like healthcare, public education, and the economy. How ambitious can we afford to be in wide-open, public spaces? Let's have a look:

Example 2: Social and Public Ecosystems (the Challenge of Tapping "Experts"). Reflect for a moment on the structural challenges facing public education and healthcare. Our best experts have come up short on solutions in spite of program after program and countless dollars of investment. I assert that the vast majority of stakeholders have proven unable—or unwilling—to collaborate.

We can paint the universe of possibilities broadly now, because I believe the fundamentals of collaboration share a common backbone, regardless of scale. Of course, we must take inventory. How many domain experts are involved? Who are the primary stakeholders, and what motivates their actions? Are the end recipients (students? patients? consumers?) playing a meaningful role in defining desired outcomes? Many of the challenges at this level of scale meet the definition of a "wicked problem," where the very definition of the problem defies consensus.[21]

Mired in political polarization and rhetoric, we lose sight of our fundamental need to find common ground.

FIGURE 3 on the next page summarizes some of the primary subject areas or *domains* where collaboration is essential on Social and Public ecosystems, in contrast to the prior commercial example. The breakdown is not intended to be complete, or to dictate how problems must be organized. In fact, there's considerable room to reposition each subject area, or connect boxes across the three columns. But a sense of the scope and scale of social ecosystem challenges begins to emerge. To take on more difficult and far-ranging problems like these means more and more people must be fundamentally better at collaborating.

FIGURE 3 – Collaboration Environments
Key places where critical collaboration efforts often fail.

Often, we simply bring in more experts. But because social problems cross many domains of expertise, those experts tend to rely on predefined solution sets for their discipline. Seemingly irresolvable conflicts emerge quickly. Definitions are ignored or remain in conflict. Working paradigms are absent, or if present in some defined or implied form, they don't align. Ideological fissures can quickly become heated sources of debate. Practitioners with strong opinions start out opposed and tend to stay that way. Facts are endlessly twisted until any hope for consensus appears futile. Add politics to the mix and the debate turns to diatribe. It's not just our inability to work together that comes under the microscope. Our inability to focus on the true sources (or root causes) of problems blocks progress. Problem-solving in these areas tends to result in gridlock. We're often debating symptoms and not causes, opinions and not facts, solutions and not problems. Gridlock happens before we get anywhere near solutions.[22]

All of this is maddeningly normal in today's marketplace of ideas. Yet we stubbornly adhere to traditional problem-solving models, even when they don't work. Let's look at one more example. This time, we'll create a hypothetical scenario, with some critical thinking on the implications of FIGURE 3.

Example 3: Domain Crossover (Relationship Impacts). The dynamics in this scenario are fairly complicated:

> *Joe lives and works in an American suburb. He is a long-time employee of a well-known regional company, sends his children to local public schools, and is an active, voting, tax-paying citizen. He and his wife, Sarah, volunteer for a non-profit that is lobbying against the state's proposed change in education policy, but its legislation is supported by Frank, the president of Joe's company and Joe's immediate boss. Frank is planning to run for the state legislature next year. Joe likes his job and respects Frank, but is a bit unsure how he feels about the policy issue, and Frank's political aspirations. They've worked well together on recent projects. Frank, of course, is looking for all the support he can get.*

Let's reflect on the implications in this vignette. Joe is a stakeholder across all three areas of influence: commercial, social, and political. He is subject to the cultural forces in each domain, and more than likely has a point of view regarding the major issues within each. But in many ways, the reality of Joe and Frank's professional working relationship means Joe and Frank are at cross purposes. This simple vignette provides a glimpse into the nature of problems in our highly interconnected 21st Century world. When we talk about the desire to collaborate, we must grapple with complex relationships like these, and ultimately, make sure we are intentional in our choices. Conventional organizational wisdom, of course, is that politics in the enterprise is a topic that's off-limits.

The problem is thus "solved" by not dealing with it.

Let's ignore conventional wisdom for a moment, and ask a few more probing questions. Does Joe reach out to Frank about the legislation or play it safe? And if Joe were to take the chance, in what contexts might Frank consider Joe's input: as an employee? Or a voter who might help him get elected? Is Joe the model engaged citizen? Or the parent of the kid down the street who cheerfully delivers his paper at 6:30 sharp every morning? Joe and Frank may be on the verge of becoming new collaborators, possibly even friends.[23] And though Frank and Joe could accomplish much together, if Joe plays it safe, neither of them may ever tap that potential.

The ability to navigate relationships, working across corporate, entrepreneurial and professional silos, brings important challenges into focus, regardless of the structure of the boxes on the chart, or the column in which such boxes might fall.

Unpacking some of the complex interactions like the ones described here is essential for social and public collaboration scenarios where connections are the most intertwined, and where it's often difficult to understand the factors having the most influence on outcomes. While the story of Joe and Frank is only a simple thought exercise, it can help us understand the relational dynamics in play. The visual is useful too; FIGURE 3 can serve as a *reference model* to help us visualize the relationships that we're talking about. Before complexity thinking came along, cause-and-effect thinkers would throw up their hands at these situations, declaring the problems too interconnected to attempt to solve (we'll discuss complexity in a bit more detail in Chapter 21). Slowly, the rules are changing.

Intentional collaboration allows us to frame the problems outlined here in solvable ways, letting collaborators work from the bottom up or the inside out to solve problems, with less reliance on direction coming from the top-down.[24] We can't solve for every context simultaneously; that would be trying to "boil the ocean." But we can, in fact, focus on those contexts that matter for the problem at hand.

So what would be my advice to Joe? I'd suggest to Joe that he take Frank out for coffee, to share how much he enjoys working for him and with him; that he sees great things in their future relationship as potential collaborators; that he's excited about Frank's upcoming run for office, but that *(laughing)* they may have to agree to disagree on some of the finer points in his education perspective; while on that point *(come to think of it)* if Frank wanted to know more about some alternate views, he and Sarah would be happy to have him over for dinner for a stimulating conversation; and by the way, is his newspaper getting to his door on time?

People value honesty and genuine heartfelt engagement. Joe isn't playing games or playing favorites, he's letting his boss know where he stands. He's offering to do his part to establish some common ground. And if Frank isn't interested in engaging, as is the tendency among many politicians, Joe is free to let his vote fall where it may.

For far too long people in organizations have been in stand-off mode, slaves to structure and afraid to embrace the hard but rewarding work of building relationships for the long term. In cultures that are fundamentally grounded in the manufacturing model of structure, hierarchy and efficiency, we've spent most of the last century taking the human element out of our work lives, in fear that feelings or emotions or the imperfections of workers might interfere with the machine that is Western civilization. We must let go of this faulty cultural imperative, a thought process buried deep in our mental models of business is supposed to work. The fact is, we've become quite good at looking the other way. The human element has always been there in our organizations, whether we've chosen to acknowledge it, or not.[25]

As she so often does, Margaret Wheatley brings the point home with a candid perspective of the typical work environment:

> *We try to engineer human contribution. We set clear expectations for performance ... then ask people to conform to our predictions ... we freeze them in their functions.*

Contrast that with her view of a more organic workplace model in action:

> *Organizing is a deep impulse ... opening more possibilities through new patterns of connection. We notice possibilities, we notice one another, we see a need which calls us to respond, and we organize.*[26]

The work to unlock and foster collaboration must attack this *shift from structure to flow*, an idea that's getting increasing traction, as evidenced by Wheatley, John Hagel and others.[27] Beneath it all is strong conviction—which I fully embrace— that people can develop a strong passion to work together, to create, and to grow. That's why this book is about unlocking insight and intention in the 21st Century, not creating it. The potential is already there. There are smart people everywhere we look. But our best innovators are trapped in silos, along with their great ideas. *We must seek to break the gridlock.*

Why are we Talking about DNA?

Mention DNA in a conversation and an image of genetic building blocks usually springs to mind. That's why DNA is a powerful metaphor for the core elements of collaboration, and it's a good example of a strong metaphor in action, as we'll explore later. But DNA is more than just a useful metaphor.

In biology, DNA provides the means for storing information about how an organism's cells will behave. It provides a place where structural design information can, over extended periods, make adjustments called *adaptation*. DNA is like a blueprint. It serves as the master plan. Solutions that develop from them are like adaptive cells, learning, changing, adapting from various components in response to the environment.[28] As we go forward, DNA will be an important reference point, an active mental model for how the collaborative process is structured. It helps us imagine how ideas can change in response to other ideas, adapting in response to a problem-solving environment that demands new alternatives. Like life itself, both ideas and organizations are organic.[29]

Like DNA, collaboration is a model of emergence.

To me, that means the building-block model of DNA is fundamentally robust as a collaborative reference model. Using it, we can pull partially formed concepts from a variety of disciplines as they are needed in an adaptive mode, rather than having predetermined solutions pushed upon us by experts.[30] That's new thinking. And rethinking how we think is about changing behaviors. There will be tentative steps. But to me, it's the only path forward.

Let's talk about how to get there.

2 – Thinking about Thinking

What Can We Learn?

Unpacking difficult problems—and the elusive, intertwined concepts that make them up—can present many unique challenges. Sometimes the hurdles are daunting. We prefer to deal with the clear and simple. We resist the vague and murky. By definition, abstract ideas resist quick understanding, making progress painfully slow. And history has not been on our side. For thousands of years philosophers—and more recently professional scientists—have done battle on topics like these, engaged in seemingly endless debates about the nature and limits of what we can know.[31]

No simple answers here, I'm afraid.

That doesn't mean we should surrender our analytical energies. Yet when it comes to thinking deeply, far too often we pull the plug. We disengage, finding ways to change the subject. And that spells sure defeat for collaboration and its cognitive cousin—*critical thinking*—on a variety of levels, often quite early in the problem-solving process. To me, turning away from the abstract and complex is a symptom of a world that has surrendered to easy remedies.

Across society, many have lost the will to understand.

A fundamental challenge of learning—whether pursued as formal education, informal knowledge sharing or the process of collaborating—is that our insights are under construction. The stuff we toss about during the learning process is comprised of loosely defined notions that are as yet unverified. Only portions of our dialog are supported by facts and figures. Other aspects are formative, and often wrong. Taking care to keep track of *what we know* vs. *what we believe* vs. *what we're considering* is a vital part of the process. To complicate matters, many insights in their earliest stages of development exist beyond the province of our conscious awareness, lurking as half-formed intuition in the category of a hunch.[32]

As we collaborate, the tangled processes of deep thinking require that we put down our established theories and formulas for a moment. We'll pick them up again when they're needed later. But to fully grapple with understanding, open minds are necessary. They must be uncluttered by presumptions and the deeply-held certainties of our existing paradigms. As we think about thinking, we see that it becomes a question of suspending what we think we know, so that we're able to learn new things and ultimately know more. It can be disconcerting to suspend what we've worked so long and hard to prove, but that's the reality of cross-disciplinary learning.

We need to be more comfortable with ambiguity.

There's no turning back from this. I've found the only way out is through. So let's unpack it some more.

Almost all collaborators, whether experts or not, bring insights to the table that are laced with assumptions. Some of these will have been shaped by our culture or our prevailing mindset, still others by professional training. Some simply show up out of nowhere for consideration. But regardless of the ultimate influences on our thinking, collaboration derives value from having this broad portfolio of inputs. And here's a key point, that I can't stress enough: *It's not a question of weeding out inputs that are less than perfect.* Our challenge is in taking care to sort fact from perception, separating new ideas from established ideas, culling value from the wide array of inputs continually surfaced. Ultimately, it's about *discernment*, the core skill that allows deep thinking to provide its richest rewards.

Insights take many forms. Some are facts. Some are opinions. Some are based on summarized data and research, while others are random thoughts and observations. I argue that all insights can be valuable, but the demand for critical thinking is clearly essential to navigate the nuances. In practice, I've found that raw insights are critically important building blocks for collaborative problem solving that get overlooked and are so often lost. These are the leaves in the river that wash downstream unseen.

It's difficult to describe ideas that aren't fully formed, but as we interact, we use conversation to share and receive snippets of new information. The human brain is a marvelous, mostly underutilized place where insights are filtered and new ideas are born. To solve difficult problems, collaborators must climb into that place. We must become deeper, more discerning thinkers. We must become aware that the exchange of insights and their subsequent refinement into new ideas is actually the core process for not only solving problems but also building new solutions.[33]

Many who specialize in innovation and solution design rely heavily on *ideas*—not *insights*—as they work. There is strong precedent here. Ideas are important building blocks of new solutions in any innovation model. But I argue that the insights that first emerge during a collaborative session can be immensely valuable as well, sometimes even more so. Often they'll spawn fundamentally different ideas, and different kinds of solutions that move in different directions. There are many models for attacking innovation, but I've found support for the notion of insight in the innovation process from innovative thinkers in that space.[34]

There is a very mysterious aspect to the generation of insight. As in the movie "Inception," the first moment of new insight can be all-important.[35] Part of what makes this approach to collaboration different from common innovation practice is that we're generating and exploring insights where there's even less structure and considerably more chaos, confusion, and messiness.[36] Ideas can be cataloged by type and put in a sequence, where insights tend to be random, making categorization more difficult. Many insights seem off-topic. They fail to line up or fall into clear categories.

For those who prefer order, such chaos is highly undesirable. These collaborators will expend great energy to return to a state of organization as quickly as they're allowed to attempt it. Of course the ordering and making sense of our inputs is a valuable step, at the right time. But if it happens too soon, too early in the developmental stages of collaboration, we may lose new perspectives. The domain of messiness and chaos are where much of the true power of emergent collaboration comes in. Insights—the lower level, raw, atomic level of thought—provide a rich base for sparking new ideas.

Power Tools of Deep Thinkers

The metaphor of the *power tool* is a time tested way to draw attention to approaches that deliver the greatest bang for the buck. As we wade through all the cognitive challenges required for collaboration, we will need the extra juice that a power tool implies. FIGURE 4 on the next page shows four power tools of deep thinkers that we'll be using repeatedly as we explore and unpack Collaboration DNA. To help us use these terms comfortably throughout the book, let's look at each of these in turn:

1. Abstraction. Much if not most of our life's experience is readily observable. We take comfort in things we can touch and see, and thereby know from first-hand experience. It's those other notions that swirl around us—those concepts that we describe as *abstract*, or without tangible form—that present problems of interpretation to the curious observer. Almost invariably, abstract concepts are a challenge when we seek to collaborate.

4 Power Tools of Deep Thinking	Working Definition	Where Useful in 21st Century Collaboration
Abstraction	Ability to generalize (and vice versa)	Envision general case from specifics (zoom out) Specify detail from general case (zoom in)
Context	Ability to relate	Create classification scheme Define relevant domain scope & boundaries Evaluate ideas in multiple scenarios Develop & refine required *metadata* Develop working *taxonomies*
Root Cause	Ability to discern	Evaluate contributing factors Determine impact & implications
Frameworks	Ability to create a coherent model	Define solution components Identify important patterns Expose influencing rules Compare current state to future state Analyze new & emerging paradigms Develop working *ontologies* Synthesize components into a cohesive whole Design solutions

FIGURE 4—Power Tools for Deep Thinking
Some important tools in the collaborative thinker's tool box

We first encounter the problems of abstraction as curious children, when we ask questions that elude basic logic. Children ask about why the sky looks blue (*color/perception*), what is the nature of "x" in algebra class (*variables/unknowns*), or where grandma went after her funeral (*death/soul*). We learn more about abstraction in high school and college as our language expands and our understanding of the world is enriched, fueled by both accumulated education and still more first-hand experience. But most people seem very happy to leave a rigorous discussion of the topic back in the classroom. Sorting out abstract concepts takes work—work we often tend to avoid—which is an issue in its own right. We will revisit that one in the chapters ahead.

Some say the aptitude for abstract thinking belongs to "right-brained" thinkers, a broad and interesting area of study with many voices, popularized recently by Dan Pink and others.[37] The field of neuroscience continues to yield breakthroughs at a dizzying pace, as we learn more and more about what is happening in the space between our ears.[38] But while psychologists continue their research, we must press ahead, staying focused on the practical.

How does abstraction show up in our problem solving?

Abstract entities share a common core: semantic classifications, relationships and patterns that make an abstract thing unique, and thus—in some useful way— knowable. It's a key point. We have to be able to frame abstractions in our mind. We need a way to package elusive ideas in ways that resonate for us, as well as for others.[39]

Models and simple rules can take us a long way in dealing with abstract concepts.

Sometimes a visual approach works best, which is why many appear in this book. Sometimes a simple grid will suffice to communicate the topic at hand, or sometimes a picture delivers more insight. There's considerable traction over the past decade using a *mind map*, a quick illustration of related ideas that we'd recognize from pads of paper and whiteboards in offices and conference rooms alike.[40] Creating such artifacts is fairly intuitive, even for those who would *not* call themselves artistic. We create visual aids like these often without noticing. It's an example of a natural, highly intuitive way that we work out our more complex ideas. Our subconscious minds are searching for patterns, boundaries, and relationships to help us make sense of the world around us.

2. Context. Nineteenth-century philosopher William James is generally considered the father of modern psychology. He was famous for recognizing that the ability to focus is one of the most important functions of the human mind.[41] By now, we've all witnessed how the information deluge of our modern world—made worse by the Internet and cable TV—has made focus increasingly difficult. But this does not create an easy out for collaborators. Problem-solving requires critical thinking, and critical thinking requires focus. The ability to set and hold context is a key skill, in spite of the many things competing for our attention.

Like engineers and architects, collaborators are innovators. They're designers of solutions and they're aggregators of new ideas.[42] Collaborators must be problem-solvers at an advanced level of sophistication. To be effective, they must become skilled at understanding the impact of different but related problem contexts, evaluating alternatives, and weighing options. Among their peers, collaborators must also learn to provide leadership in these areas, demonstrating how to choose among several viable paths, understanding why we're doing so, and ultimately, being prepared to explain it. When we approach a collaboration exercise, we can think of context as:

- **A set of perspectives**
- **Our analytical point of view**
- **The lens through which we view a problem**
- **A specific orientation or sense with which we comprehend something**

Significant crossover benefits come about when we're able to use multiple contextual scenarios for comparison. We must recognize context, and learn how to change it in the moment. When we've mastered the skill, we need to be able to carry it out in a group setting. It's no small task, but critical all the same.

3. Root Cause. For complex problems and challenges, the contributing factors are typically far more intertwined than any one participant or small group is able to see. Collaboration can fail outright when don't invest in the necessary rigor. The notion of *root cause analysis* is germane here. It brings a level of understanding to most debates that is so often lacking. In short, a discussion of *causality* involves the consideration of all possible source factors that may have ultimately contributed to an outcome. In my consulting work with Dr. Eric Threatt, I've see first-hand how the Ishikawa (or "fishbone") diagram provides a useful way to communicate root cause in different contexts. It visually shows how disparate factors influence a specific problem or situation.[43] A simple example of such an analysis appears as FIGURE 5.

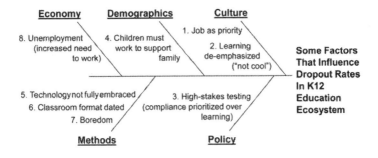

FIGURE 5—Root Cause Analysis
Evaluating insight in different contexts using
Ishikawa diagrams

Approaches like this can help challenge preconceived notions. Placing factors side by side broadens the discussion landscape. The value here is one of bringing focus. Our brains can be very efficient at eliminating competing data points or factors, resulting in gaping holes in our logic and decision making. We routinely evaluate insights that were most recently presented, making broad assumptions about their relative importance while ignoring the full picture. Categorizing those insights into related groups can help us head that off.

Some may balk at using an Ishikawa diagram along with any mention of root-cause analysis, because it harkens back to the cause-and-effect thinking that is fundamental to our old industrial mental models. It's a way of thinking that can be problematic. I agree in principal, and we need to tread carefully here. But when it comes to framing a problem, we often need the rigor and critical thinking that an Ishikawa provides. We can't be consumed by exclusive use of it, or any other specific tool. Our toolkit is large for good reason. It's a question of finding the right tool for the job. When many variables compete for our attention, tools like this can quickly provide clarity on where we must focus. In the new world of flow, this approach may prove a necessary evil, a throwback to the days of structure and control. Or it may be a tool that evolves in new and useful ways. I predict the latter.

The bottom line is that collaborative teams must own the comprehensive view, and not slip into the many and varied traps associated with incremental thinking. Understanding causality is at the core of this.

4. Frameworks. Let's define *frameworks* as simple mental tools that help us model our abstract ideas. Out in the real world, we desperately need ways to capture and communicate what we're thinking. A framework helps us achieve that. When we embrace simple conceptual models, useful concepts like boundaries, patterns and business rules come along for the ride. It's conceptual scaffolding that helps us hold our ideas together while we're hard at work figuring out how the pieces might fit together. The notion of optional, changeable configurations implied by the metaphor is a powerful one. *To optimize our learning potential, our cognitive scaffolding must remain portable.*

A key aspect of learning to use frameworks is how we capture our ideas and represent their patterns and rules. What are the flows that are important in our conceptual model? Who are the stakeholders?

How does the system—or ecosystem—function?

We need simple ways to foster more rigorous interactions of the ideas we are developing, creating both common ground and focus. We need an approach that increases our chances for getting more smart people focused on our common objectives. This includes gaining consensus more quickly and more consistently. As we expand our ability to drive innovation and change, a leap in productivity and the quality of our collaborative outcomes looks more realistic. With focus, coordination and rigor, we're literally working toward getting smarter, faster.[44]

Most scientific disciplines, for example, have rules and theories called *epistemologies* that provide an over-arching framework for how things are generally believed to function. While these are immensely important frameworks that guide entire fields of scientific research and development—as well providing the basis for our modern education systems— academic paradigms can work against the creative process. The concept of *paradigm blindness* has the power to create mental gridlock, literally blocking new thinking.[45]

I believe simple collaboration frameworks for problems and solutions helps us more easily establish a baseline for what modern organizations are attempting to achieve. Developing new, simple frameworks and solution models also improves our ability to adapt. We must be more flexible in framing what we can know, and always remain willing to reframe it, even if it means starting over. This helps us move away from recurring and familiar debates about process, domain expertise, and the way things work in silos, academic ones, or otherwise.

With flexible scaffolding, we find many more possibilities. It's less and less about choosing sides among experts, picking a solution from a pre-printed catalog. That's a win-lose proposition does not serve our collaborative ends. The better path is to shed the old mental models, finding a new patch of common ground upon which to construct our new ideas. Solution frameworks are most readily modeled as changes to the current framework. That's an important simplifying assumption as we formulate our thinking. We can think of problems and solutions in pairs: old/new, current/future, before/after or, as IT consultants like me like to say: "as is" and "to be". In the design process, alternative solutions begin to emerge; those that stick are full solutions. If there are breakthrough results, many would call these final outputs *innovations*.[46]

Now, perhaps, we're starting to see how teams can solve difficult problems together armed with a few power tools and conventions. We create a shared view of the problem, and use it to iterate toward one or more shared solutions. Abstraction is attacked head on, to help us consider general design scenarios separately from actual solutions. Context shifts by group consensus, evaluating different factors that apply in different situations. Understanding causal relationships helps us navigate facts from theories, and helping us establish relevance. Simple frameworks provide the scaffolding that holds our ideas together while we develop them.

If we stay focused on our approach to this work and bring rigor to the mix, we have a chance at becoming better as collaborators, possibly in the not-so-distant future. Things are getting a bit more interesting. The ability to solve problems in teams may be less daunting than we'd first concluded.

So what are collaboration's practical possibilities?

It's time to talk about results, the tangible outputs that might be created by a group working together to solve problems. What do our results look like? What outcomes can we imagine, guide and help create?

Let's tackle that next.

3 – Outcomes

What Can We Achieve?

In our fast-paced age of instant answers, we often go to the Internet to start searching for solutions before we've defined the problems. I've caught myself doing this as well. The speed of response from the typical search engine makes us sloppy. We blindly guess at what might be relevant keywords. And if we're close, depending on the topic, we might get lucky. Google even has a "Feeling lucky?" link for the more impetuous among us for precisely that sentiment.

But in keeping with our new sense of focus and rigor, we have to challenge ourselves.

Are we asking the right questions?

What is our intent?

In the last chapter, we moved through examples of purposeful, coordinated evaluation of inputs that gave us a basis for problem solving. We explored ways to handle those that were more abstract, and discussed the notion of context for evaluating them.

In this chapter, we'll focus on the outputs.

It may be sobering to realize that our ability to frame and discuss abstract subject matter is generally not deliverable by Internet search. True, there are great articles and books to be found, and thousands of online, blog-based debates with fascinating twists and turns; these can offer rich sources to fuel our collaborative efforts. In fact, Internet search is great for finding answers to problems that have already been solved, surfacing relevant insights that can serve as key inputs to our work. But that's not the same as bringing rigor to our how frame our problems, which is fundamental to our ability to produce new and original outputs.

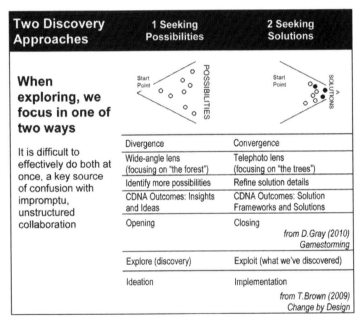

Two Discovery Approaches	1 Seeking Possibilities	2 Seeking Solutions
When exploring, we focus in one of two ways		
It is difficult to effectively do both at once, a key source of confusion with impromptu, unstructured collaboration	Divergence	Convergence
	Wide-angle lens (focusing on "the forest")	Telephoto lens (focusing on "the trees")
	Identify more possibilities	Refine solution details
	CDNA Outcomes: Insights and Ideas	CDNA Outcomes: Solution Frameworks and Solutions
	Opening	Closing
		from D. Gray (2010) Gamestorming
	Explore (discovery)	Exploit (what we've discovered)
	Ideation	Implementation
		from T. Brown (2009) Change by Design

FIGURE 6 – Two Modes of Focus in Collaborative Discovery
Different ways to describe our investigations

Today's more difficult problems demand that we define the issues more carefully, moving beyond simple facts and figures and pre-packaged insights served up by search engines.

In terms of viable outcomes, what is possible?

Photographers know that changing focus with a camera lens generally falls into one of two categories: telephoto, which is used for more detail, and wide-angle, used to zoom out to see more subject matter. When collaborating, we will need to do both: focusing on specifics to refine a solution versus broadening our investigation to identify new possibilities. Both are important in the learning and problem solving process including, for example, learning to play a new game.[47]

A collaborating team must be aware of which mode they're using. I've found it best not to jump back and forth in the same conversation; it can confuse the conversation at best and prove utterly disruptive, at worst. FIGURE 6 explores some scenarios that align with these two modes of focusing. The refinement of problems and solutions alike must undergo both modes of analysis. Collaborators need to determine the most relevant and efficient mode of discovery for the topic at hand.

An impressive inventory of analytical techniques is used by innovation practitioners and consultants alike. But if we take out differences stemming from purpose, format and style, the vast majority of them fall into these two general modes of analysis.[48] Whether we're zooming in or out, our common objective is the discovery of something we didn't know before, which is a good definition for a *collaboration outcome*.

Let's be more specific. Here are the four possible *outputs* that can emerge from a successful collaborative session:

- **Insights.** New thoughts generated quickly and easily in most collaboration settings, but often lost. Since insights serve as the raw material for ideas, the best ones should be compiled and indexed for subsequent use whenever possible. They serve as the cross-bars and platforms of the scaffolding that's necessary to build-up and support emerging ideas.

- **Ideas.** The result of reviewing insights in various contexts to identify and establish components of a new solution. This is accomplished by evaluating both ideas and insights against one another, linking them together in different contexts, or comparing ideas with other ideas to determine possible contributions to a solution.

- **Solution Framework (including Models and Paradigms).** A set of conceptual ideas and supporting insights combined with governing rules and patterns of interaction to address the problem or topic in a general way.

- **Solutions (or Innovations).** A final deliverable that's a significant improvement over prior practice; it's something that can be done, achieved, or built; and it's often (but not always) modeled on a Solution Framework but in every case, something for which a plan could be created to implement.

The process of collaboration—like learning and knowledge sharing—is iterative, so the outputs of any one collaboration or project can be inputs to the next. This is a critical dynamic of an organic flow which we should keep in mind.

Many collaborative teams want to focus exclusively on ideas and there's significant historical precedent for this approach.[49] But as I said in Chapter 2, there's a need for some caution here. Starting with preset ideas can be a dangerous constraint, limiting our perceived choices. We can easily make assumptions about available options that short-cut objective critical thinking. An "ideas only" focus can allow us to bypass the hard work of solution definition, design, and qualification, and we can end up choosing from a series of ill-defined scenarios, often out of context. This happens because stock ideas are often borrowed wholesale from elsewhere, but they arrive with limited information on approach and circumstances.

A great example in K12 Education is the seemingly endless debate on the viability and relative wisdom of charter schools. In short, this approach represents an alternative funding model to public education. Public funds are used without traditional policy constraints, as a means of fostering local innovation. From there, the scenarios allowed by various states and attempted by various organizers are incredibly diverse.

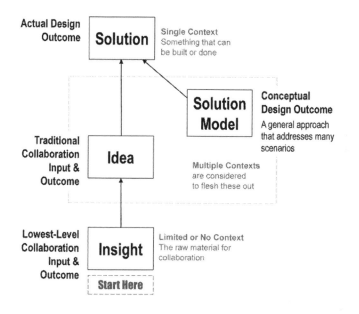

FIGURE 7 – Possibilities: Taxonomy of Outcomes

Comparing the potential results of a collaborative effort in a structured way; identifies the role of *context* in creating useful relationships

A broad range of variables is in play. That means a generic conversation on the pros and cons of charters, without establishing context, is generally unproductive, if not meaningless. Without sufficient information, we can't ground the proposed idea as a solution in practical terms, and we have no way of knowing whether it might be viable. Some charters do quite well, though we'd never know it by skimming the headlines.[50] And yet the debates rage on.

Pre-conceived insights, ideas and even existing solutions (when qualified and put in context) can serve as valuable inputs—*this has been tried before, and here's how it worked*—becoming new fodder for collaboration. But this is not an alternative to objective critical thinking. Is the topic at hand going to help address my problem?

Context is how we determine relevance.

FIGURE 7 summarizes the relationship of collaboration possibilities that we'll also refer to as outcomes. We'll come back to these terms and concepts often (consult the Glossary if the terms still aren't as clear.) What might we derive from this chart? Again, in practice, we tend to start at the top, with solutions. We live in a world that rushes to answers. Perhaps this is due to our test-saturated education, our achievement-oriented culture, or maybe it's simply due to our lack of time. Or perhaps the rush is built into our work flows, derived from business models to beat the competition to market. Those incredibly powerful, high-speed Internet search engines don't help, fueling our bias to go straight to available answers. There's a perception of implied urgency that profoundly influences our behavior. Let's break the curse. Harvesting the value of effective, creative, and innovative collaboration requires starting at the lowest level of our thought processes, the place where the raw material of our collaboration emerges. When we start with and track the key insights, we allow new ideas to form from them. Too often we start with full-blown ideas or solutions and argue their benefits without taking quality time to consider the full implications of the problem.

Another challenge collaborators face is the common tendency to bypass the solution model or framework step completely. "We haven't got time for frameworks or models," the argument goes, "we need to move to implementation." Unfortunately, the framework or model serves as the design template for the final solution. Bypassing the critical thinking that goes into the model is tantamount to "winging it," which severely reduces the chance of achieving desired results.

Shortcuts, unfortunately, are popular. When it comes to a fast-track mindset, we must proceed with caution. The notion that we already have the viable solutions is at the core of paradigm blindness, the tendency for experts to stay within the confines of established academic knowledge, casting aside the need to look further.[51]

Mapping Problems to their Outcomes	Problem Domains for Comparison		
	Business Model Change (Commercial)	K12 or Health Care Reform (Social Ecosystem)	Community Development or NFP-NGO* (Public Ecosystem)
Collaboration OUTCOMES (from FIGURE 7)	Market change demands new approach	Current system struggles to meet 21st Century needs	Lack of stakeholder engagement
Insights	• Stakeholder Feedback • Research Findings	• Trend Data • Practitioner & Stakeholder Feedback • Research Findings	• Testimonials
Ideas	• Competitive Analysis • Focus Group Brainstorms	• #ECOSYS Brainstorms • Bright Spots • Case Studies • White Papers	• Community Forum Brainstorms • Case Studies
Solution Models	• Scenarios	• Scenarios • New Paradigms	• Scenarios • Stakeholder Models
Solutions	• Specific Proposals	• Specific Proposals • Legislative Reforms • New Programs	• Specific Proposals • Legislation • Fundraising Plans & Templates

*NFP=Non-Profits
NGO=Non-Governmental Organizations

FIGURE 8 – Examples of Collaboration Outcomes
What might we produce using Collaboration DNA?

FIGURE 8 provides examples for outcomes as defined in this chapter. What can we make of this table? Even simple models and frameworks will vary based on need, situation, and the preferences of the collaborating team. Effective collaborators are those who are able to think and choose frameworks as they progress in problem/solution development. They must make such decisions in real time, without being afraid of being wrong, imperfect, or needing to start over.

True learning means being willing to make mistakes, a scenario which many are not yet ready to embrace. The reality of collaboration, like the process of knowledge generation itself, is one of iteration, with ideas emerging from insights in cycles.

On the next page, FIGURE 9 shows how the components of Collaboration DNA interact in a series of flows.[52] This model ties together the primary building blocks we'll continue to discuss throughout the book. The outcomes (black boxes) in FIGURE 9 are identical to the four outlined earlier in this chapter, FIGURES 7 and 8, which means our Framework is coherent. FIGURE 9 is designed to answer a different question:

How can we visualize the flow of insight when collaborating, and how might we iterate toward more tangible outcomes?

Like all reference models, FIGURE 9 should drive discussion and understanding, rather than serving as a prescriptive recipe. Collaboration is built upon iterative progressions of understanding, which this diagram reflects. Our thoughts turn over and over in our heads as we repeatedly reshape them, in hopes that something beneficial will emerge. In collaborative settings, this happens among group members, and repeats as often as the group decides it is warranted. FIGURE 9 does *not* show the specific process steps required for collaboration. In fact, all of the specific steps that take place in a collaborative session would fall inside the gray box *Intentional Collaboration.* This detail will be covered later when we explore the many nuances that wrap around a process that depends on flow. For now, simply follow the basic threads in this model to see how the collaboration process might evolve in different ways each time. Start in the lower left, as insights are first generated, then considered. Note the many branches. Note the paths that loop back to the beginning. Note that some paths are optional. This model is consistent with academic views on the value of adaptive feedback loops and how knowledge emerges through interactive contact.[53] This diagram marks a transition. Think of FIGURE 9 as a stepping stone, as we move from Part 1, framing the problem-solving challenges we face in the 21st Century, to Parts 2-4, discussing the many interesting dynamics of collaboration.

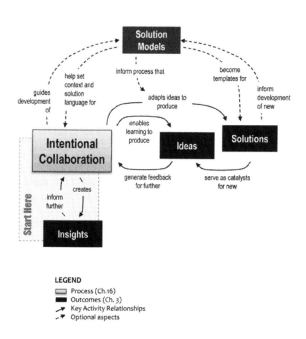

FIGURE 9 – Visualizing the Flow of Insights
A reference model for visualizing Collaborative Outcomes
*(to download a full PDF version of this reference model,
go to http://collaborationdna.com)*

PART 2: MESSAGING

"Language shapes
perception. What
we see is what
we're prepared to
see."

Peter Senge

4 – Intention

When it comes to solving problems in teams, do you ever wonder about the motivations of others? What about your own? Perhaps you've found yourself at some point going through the motions for something important, especially if it involved working with a group? Even if we profess a commitment to quality follow-through and helping out the team, we struggle to find and allocate the necessary time to truly engage. There simply aren't enough hours in the day.

More and more, we settle for the rush job.

Collaborators need to grapple with these challenges, because groups looking for quick answers are unlikely to make the investments necessary for collaborative success. There are several basic questions that can help us battle the "hurry-up" onslaught, bringing deeper focus to the tasks at hand and giving us more genuine insight that can help us navigate the day-to-day noise of confusing and conflicting priorities. Some tough questions need to be asked:

- **Why are we doing this?**
- **What is the desired outcome of this effort?**
- **How can we get the job done in a quality fashion, marshaling our talents and energies to the task?**
- **Can we rationalize this with other priorities?**
- **Do we need help?**

If you and your team members can't provide clear answers to these questions, it's doubtful the group is fully engaged. What's more, it's doubtful much will get done, in spite of surface-level appearances and a full host of people occupying seats at the table. Showing up is not the same as adding value. Commitment has deep roots that aren't always visible to casual observers. Eventually, a good leader will know if you're committed, because sensing and building commitment is part of their job. To me, with time and resources ever more scarce, the best course is to take the mystery out of the equation. Get down to brass tacks. If you explore your own internal motivations, you can probably help the rest of the group get to a collective answer more quickly.

"I'm here because of X ... what about you?"

Insist on heartfelt, authentic answers. If you don't like the answers, it's time to reevaluate the task at hand, perhaps brainstorming other ways that it might better be achieved. Collaborative efforts need everyone's input, but the focus should be on 100% investment. Step up, or step aside, but by all means, take a step. If you do, the rest of the group will notice and follow suit.

What many collaborators lack, in a word, is intention.

There's really no getting off the hook. As individuals, we're ultimately accountable for our willingness to focus, to invest time, and to engage more fully and more deeply to help those around us. We can and do own the choices in front of us.[54]   The group dynamic will feed from individual commitments.

Collaboration fails when a majority of contributors are merely going through the motions. Some excel at putting a good face on it, playing well-rehearsed roles to meet expectations without really trying. Some might be malicious and even manipulative in their role-playing, creating the appearance of collaboration to achieve another agenda, a behavior often tagged *passive aggressive*.

Still others, and from my experience this is a greater percentage of the crowd, will be completely unaware of their lack of investment. After too many years spent in pointless meetings and committees talking in circles, they've grown used to passive participation. They accept organizational time-wasting as the status quo. They'll show up, answer questions when asked, and then leave.

Whatever the cause, the result is the same.

No engagement? No collaboration. No results.

Again, we'll take on the broader systemic and environmental issues in the pages ahead. For now let's keep exploring closer to home. What is behind these personal motivation issues?

Margaret Wheatley makes an interesting point about human survival instincts: "while we are free to choose, we choose on the basis of self."[55] While this sounds like an unappealing, fundamentally selfish motivation, I believe her thought is grounded in basic human nature. Using updates to Maslow's classic "Hierarchy of Needs" model as a reference point, survival and safety come first; addressing the needs of others, including belonging and gaining esteem, are secondary needs, and are not as deeply held.[56] It's interesting that helping to achieve the greater good of the organization (or society in general) do not appear in the hierarchy, in either its original or updated form.

That begs the question: what is our true motivation when we opt-in for a collaborative exercise? What is it we're trying to accomplish?

As we move up Maslow's original pyramid, there is clearly attention to affinity and belonging—the desire to be a part of something bigger than ourselves—but I believe that simply accounts for our social energy, our desire for contact and support from others. For additional "higher order" collaboration motivators that take us into the dynamics of team problem solving, we must look outside Maslow, into the area of personal growth.

Carol Dweck introduces a highly relevant argument for modern motivation in *Mindset* (2006). She describes a fundamental divide between people who believe their skills and talents are predetermined (or *fixed*) vs. those who believe they can advance their stake in the world by effort and learning (through *growth*). Through her research she's convinced that those with a fixed mindset are primarily focused on being perceived as successful, having good answers, and ultimately avoiding embarrassment, generally taking a defensive or evasive posture on matters of critical thinking. With a growth mindset, in contrast, Dweck finds people who are motivated learners, willing to take risks and using mistakes to learn more.[57] She argues that a growth mindset will provide the necessary frame of mind for taking chances.

Dweck says much of this orientation is acquired in our youth, influenced greatly by parents and teachers. And, while a fixed mindset and its many deep-seated biases can be unlearned and changed over time, shifting to a new mindset as adults can prove time-consuming. The degree to which people embrace new thinking is very deeply entrenched in feelings of self-worth, feelings that are often reinforced over decades.

Another perspective on behavior in the workplace comes from Chris Argyris, a deep and candid observer on the negative effects of fear in an organization. Argyris spent many years examining how people in different companies behave and was able to distill clear tendencies within organizations that suppress information. These tendencies included the avoidance of certain issues, and creating environments that would, in the name of protecting the status quo and ensuring the survival of the collective, serve to thwart the knowledge sharing that collaboration requires.[58]

The research of Chris Argyris resonated strongly with me when I learned of it, but I was a bit discouraged when I realized that it was published over 30 years ago. Some news doesn't travel so fast, even with the help of the Internet. Organizational dynamics are complex and challenging, resistant to change, and difficult to influence.

In many ways, we've always known. I often call it "smart people behaving badly."

Change, I believe, starts with individuals who embrace collaboration intentionally. They insist on a collaborative approach as a ticket to earning their involvement. And organizations whose leaders embrace collaboration as a requirement have the best chance of all, because the hard work of team-based problem solving gains an important mandate.

What can we do about this in team settings? We need to get intention issues on radar and addressed at the very beginning, when resources are being allocated to the effort and commitments are being made. For the individual, there's work to do at two-levels: private promises that you make to yourself *("I will work through my reservations, and will find ways to make this successful")* and the commitments you are asked to make to others *("You've convinced me, I'm in!").*

This is a key point that is routinely missed. The only viable time to ask tough questions like the ones above— especially if you expect honest answers—is before starting. Downstream, the likelihood of face-saving comments, peer pressure and momentum-based inertia will likely mask deeper feelings. If there is hesitation, ask people if they want to opt out, or merely observe, or play supporting roles. But don't wait. Asking these questions downstream is too late.

With difficult problems, we're often talking about the need for some high-stakes engagement, which can bring some personal risk. We need to assess our readiness to lead change.

Is everyone on board? Are we committing 100%?

Let's face it: working with others can be time-consuming. We face the logistical hurdles of assembling a group and keeping members focused. Herding cats takes time. There is the challenge of translating terminology across different areas, and the significant challenge of gaining (and maintaining) consensus. We'll tackle these topics in upcoming chapters, but the bottom line is that collaboration will be work; lots of work. If we're going to be successful, collaboration must be a high priority. We're going to genuinely need to want it.

Another destructive factor is the lurking suspicion among some in the group that, "It would be easier to just do this by myself." We've probably all gone there. We may not have been aware of the implication or been proud of the conclusion, but this simple, commonplace thought is often the result of frustration. Unfortunately, this bias can quickly become pervasive, deeply influencing how we think, serving to sabotage any commitment to participate intentionally.

If you truly believe this sentiment, you'll usually feel as if you're wasting your own time. You'll likely become either combative or "checked-out." There's a partial truth at work here, in the sense that we probably could get to some answers or produce outcomes *faster* on our own, but in this self-centered calculus we're ignoring breadth, quality, and comprehensiveness of solution. Again, we should challenge our thought process. Are we able to work openly and seamlessly with others? Do we believe that working in groups is desirable? Do we respect the contributions of others? Do we trust that others will hear us fairly and objectively, and not judge our contributions? The option of "going solo" essentially reduces the collaborative equation to one of efficiency ("time to achieve answers") while ignoring overall effectiveness ("quality of answers"). We trade impact for speed. We sacrifice the long-term objective for a short-term win.

The priority in this case, perhaps, is checking the box and moving on.

Most arrive at this relatively cynical place from experience, having endured numerous failed attempts at collaboration. Chalk it up to endless and pointless corporate or civic committee meetings, or the political gridlock that so routinely blocks fervent attempts for people who were sincerely trying to work together. We'll find throughout *The DNA of Collaboration* that we have much to unlearn.

It's time for a fresh start, to take the leap of faith that collaboration in a team setting can actually work.

- **How badly do we want a quality result?**
- **How much do we want to make a difference?**
- **Are we willing to work for it?**
- **Are we prepared to identify and achieve levels of effort that 100% commitment truly means?**

Intention serves to unlock your inner voice of commitment. Intentional collaboration requires a clear, affirmative message: *"As individuals within this group, we're committed to delivering solutions as a team, doing what it takes to make this collaboration work."* It's not far-fetched for collaborators to post these words on a wall as a not-so-gentle reminder. Human nature, years of negative experience, and the many challenges we'll explore in the pages ahead produce a strong drag on new thinking and new behavior.

Intentional collaboration requires 100%.

How do we know when we are ready? For any team to reach its full potential, it's important to level-set in on its current capabilities, relative to what it must strive to achieve. Quantifying that, of course, is a challenge. How big is the gap in each area?

I've developed a simple Collaboration Readiness framework, shown in FIGURE 10, which shows eight vectors for success in intentional collaboration. A team may elect to define more or fewer vectors, by grouping them differently. What I especially like about this approach is that a diagram like this can be drawn (and re-drawn) on a white board in moments, and team contributions can be surfaced quickly. For groups serious about solving difficult problems, the process of defining "100%" and their gap to achieve it is valuable. It helps us set healthy expectations, and it lets us know where there's work to be done. What's important is that each team looks at its capabilities and is honest with its assessment. It's also important not to assign numerical scores or to call out individuals within the team.

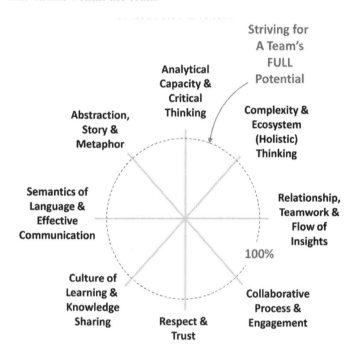

FIGURE 10 – A Collaboration Readiness Framework
Eight vectors to evaluate a group's collaboration maturity

In practice, all that's needed is a single point on each vector, representing the group's collective progress on the road to 100%. Targeting "100%" is relative and a bit arbitrary, but that's by design. Each team can grow to its own potential, as it defines success for itself. A group that's beginning to assess its collaboration potential will plot a point on each vector, representing progress toward a 100% goal. Two sample points are shown as FIGURE 11.

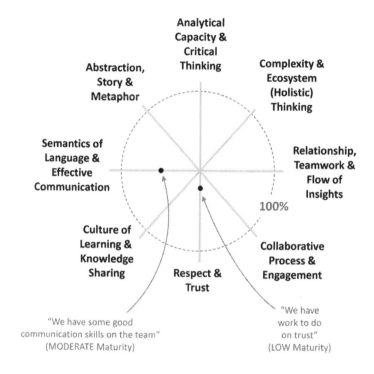

FIGURE 11 – Using the Readiness Framework
Placing a data point on each vector "scores" the group's relative maturity *(note: this model will be discussed further in Chapter 18, once each area of Collaboration DNA is fully explored)*

Ultimately, we'll establish a point on all eight vectors, connect the dots, and plan a strategy to further maximize our performance. I'll walk through some scenarios for that in Chapter 18. But first, in the chapters ahead, we'll delve into substance of each dimension, learning what's implied by each vector and establishing a practical appreciation for how we can achieve success.

TAKEAWAYS for "Intention"

To challenge your thinking and level of progress in this important area, ask yourself the following questions:

T1. In team settings, can we detect (a.) going thru motions vs. (b.) acting from deep conviction? Can asking 'why' be enough to surface intention? What is a better way to ensure our intentions are clear?

T2. Wheatley and Maslow tell us survival is a primal motivator. In business, how does this impact our willingness to take risks?

T3. Dweck says learning & risk-taking are easy when we have a growth mindset vs. obsessing on our perceived fixed limitations. Have you seen this play out for yourself or others you know?

T4. The 21st century seems to demand focus on quick wins over longer-term goals. Can both be achieved? What's the ultimate priority?

As with many questions that arise during collaboration, not all will have a right or wrong answer. To younger generations raised in a season of high-stakes testing, this ambiguity will present some uncomfortable moments. Such is the challenge of critical thinking, which we'll continue to unpack in the chapters ahead.

Note: From here on, as we explore actionable approaches for collaboration, I'll end each chapter with a set of questions to help frame takeaways; my goal is to stimulate thoughts on how the material might best be applied.

5 – Choosing Our Words

The Semantics of Being Understood

Language plays a subtle but deeply powerful role in how we engage with others. Yet we're so completely immersed in our minute-by-minute trafficking of words in their myriad combinations that we scarcely give language a second thought. If we reflect on how we think about, evaluate, and come to understand virtually anything, we realize that the running voice of our conscious thought sets practical boundaries. We can only explain problems and solutions to the degree that we have words for them.[59]

Language, it seems, binds our possibilities.[60]

But it's a two-sided coin; on the other side there is an enabler: words are the raw materials of new ideas. Our language is the foundation for what we are capable of creating together. For every scenario where our words prove limiting, there are still others where words that could serve to unlock new ideas.

I'll argue that our ability to communicate clearly and efficiently is perhaps the most important aspect of collaboration. How good are we at explaining our position? Do we know if we're being understood? How long does it take to get our point across (assuming, of course, that we ever get there)? From nearly 30 years of working to improve the effectiveness of collaborative teams, I've found the challenges associated with communication are fundamental. For most of us it's too late now, but I have concluded one thing:

We should have paid more attention in English class.

The problem exists at many levels. Too often, people talk past each other, haphazardly using words that hold no meaning for the listener, or worse, using words that have obscure meanings *by design*. If we choose to collaborate, we are choosing to be understood. It goes with the territory. But recognizing that a gap exists isn't enough. People rarely take the time to choose their words. Definitions are loose, sloppy, or altogether absent. The results can be disastrous.

One of the great thinkers on the topic of language is Ludwig Wittgenstein. He argued that the failure to reconcile conflicting views in philosophy and science could be traced to mishandling of words and their meanings; he is famous for exposing the futility of debates between great thinkers who had, from his perspective, not bothered to define key terms.[61] To me, this is a frightening insight. If brilliant academic luminaries and thinkers have been dropping the semantic ball for centuries, what chance do the rest of us have?

I'll stay optimistic, for one primary reason: language is a skill that can always be improved, once we focus in on the problem and come to terms with it. A time-tested approach is to expand contact with books, pushing our reading lists to include more difficult and involved fiction, with special focus on topics extending beyond our own experience. As we read more, our vocabularies expand, our understanding and command of the language grows, and our communication improves. But that's no place to stop. In truth it's only the beginning.

The next level of improvement involves more focused semantic awareness in real-time situations.

Here are some sound bites that demonstrate semantic rigor in action:

- **"I tend to define that very differently."**
- **"Don't forget, many words have different meanings when used in different contexts."**
- **"Let's look it up."**
- **"Maybe we can define a common working definition that fits our problem/solution context."**

I always try to advocate setting aside time to define key terms. The relatively brief amount of overhead pays huge dividends. It not only improves the quality of collaborative efforts, it can literally save an ill-fated collaboration from tumbling into semantic sink holes fed by strong differences of opinion.

Challenges quickly emerge when experts from one field use the same terms in different ways. For example, the word *hypothesis* in mathematics means something different (an assumption, or a given) than it does in science (a theory to be proven). This is the kind of detail that's easily missed, at the expense of productive collaboration.

For better or worse, the language we use and the communication that follows reflects our deepest thought processes. But the benefit isn't always the listener's. Peter Senge extended the foundational thinking of quantum physicist David Bohm when he argued that a close, symbiotic flow exists between our thoughts and our words, "Language shapes perception. What we see depends on what we're prepared to see."[62]

How deep do our deepest thought processes extend? That tends to be a function of our willingness and skill to engage in critical thinking. Whenever we communicate, there are actually far greater implications to our ideas than may be evident in our spoken words. Context and subtext conspire to give our ideas deeper meaning, sometimes whether we're consciously aware of it or not. When we use a combination of specific words to make a point, state an idea, or advance some sort of proposition, there is almost always a much larger meaning implied, like an iceberg, hidden beneath the surface, as shown in FIGURE 12.

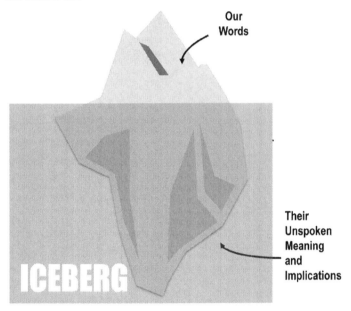

FIGURE 12 – Ideas are like Icebergs
Our intended meaning (beneath the surface) is typically much more expansive than the actual words we use

One job of collaborators is to expose the meaning of our ideas and propositions quickly and effectively, rather than leaving team members guessing or at a loss as to what you're trying to say. Again, awareness of semantic differences is not always enough to resolve the language problem. Domain experts are often deeply entrenched in their terminology. After all, many earned advanced degrees and have spent entire careers in an effort to master their discipline. Moving outside our own professional domain of expertise can be uncomfortable for all parties.

How might we combat this?

I've had success using the concept of *solution language* to create common ground, an idea I tapped from the writings of Clayton Christensen.[63] In effect, the collaborators agree on working definitions that are essentially a mash-up of different perspectives and disciplines. This is not a short-cut or rule-breaking exercise, but rather, a powerful means of building consensus. When a team is able to co-create a small solution to remove a barrier, the sense of partnership and team-work is palpable. Early wins are important. Here are some more sure signs of progress, working to build a coherent and resilient semantic framework:

- **"What happens if we redefine the problem?"**
- **"Are we in agreement on all terms?"**
- **"If we agree to that, does it resolve the debate so we can move forward?"**
- **"We've developed several definitions unique to our effort; let's create a project glossary"**

These statements demonstrate that the wheels of semantic alignment are turning. Many, many collaborations fail because they never reach this simple set of milestones. Simple negotiation may be the answer in some cases. But often a more rigorous analysis and semantic structure are called for, especially for the most complex, cross-disciplinary problems.

Two semantic frameworks come to our rescue most readily. The first, the concept of *taxonomy,* was put into early use by Aristotle and has had perhaps its most recognizable use in biology, in no small part owing to Aristotle himself.[64] Most of us will recall the nested hierarchy of plant and animal species, describing the order of things in a rigorous attempt to classify the world. But the value of a well-designed taxonomy can extend beyond biology or social sciences like sociology.

Business and academic practitioners of *knowledge management*—an approach that seeks to improve organizational learning—employs taxonomies to define the hierarchy of core concepts in a business environment. Information Technology (or "IT") departments will sometimes develop an Information Architecture using a taxonomy construct. This approach can be helpful to show the flow of a web application, the universe of *metadata* for tagging and drop-down lists, or to clarify relationships of key terms across the organization.

While the semantic rigor of defining key words can be helpful, taking time to model the whole world—or even just an entire business—can be like trying to boil the ocean. The relative value of modeling business terms is often debated. I believe the strongest value enters in when new concepts or solutions are being defined, or where significant divisions emerge about how to describe important concepts. In these cases, building reference taxonomies can help. Examples so far include FIGURES 3 and 7.

Another useful way to model the world around us is to use a modeling approach called *ontology*. Strictly defined, it's a model of things that exist in the world. But it broadens the scope of taxonomy by describing relationships or interactions among the components. To create one is a process of placing action statements or a description of each relationship between elements in the model. A good working example is FIGURE 9.

With just a small amount of focus and rigor, we've upped the ante. We've moved beyond simple semantic definitions and we're starting to address how words interact in complex ways. Gradually, as we communicate, these semantic models help us to see new insights, creating the scaffolding that helps us construct still more fully-developed ideas. We're assembling the tools we'll need to foster emergent thinking, laying out the building blocks for effective collaboration.

From a traditional design perspective we're not treading on new ground, but we are crossing domains a bit. In the IT arena, as we touched on above, models like these are common. An object model helps describe the ontological elements of a new system; a data model is a bit of a hybrid, proving more static than a pure ontology, but with more information about unique aspects of relationship than a traditional hierarchical taxonomy. Enter any IT shop in corporate America, and you'll find simple models like the ones described above scrawled on every whiteboard in the place. Mastering the modeling techniques themselves is not the primary objective here. Instead, what we're after is a new awareness—and a willingness—to contemplate our ideas in useful, often visual, ways.

Simple semantic models help us understand each other.

The actual need for such models in practice depends on the complexity of the problem. Social ecosystems like education or healthcare raise the bar considerably when it comes to semantics, because the issues invariably cross disciplines. Revisit the domains defined in FIGURES 2 and 3. In practice, collaboration often sparks deeply heated semantic debates across these boundaries. Building a working taxonomy or ontology allows us to define problem and solution components in new, agreed-upon ways.

The cross-disciplinary challenge points to another tricky spot in navigating semantics. Just how precise do we expect our words to be? Can't there be value in celebrating the variety of our words and our language? The short answer is *yes*.

Many celebrate the ambiguity of words—poets, novelists, and deep thinkers among them—valuing the twists and turns that our language affords. As a writer, I share the enthusiasm. But when solving problems, semantic clarity is like a gate on the pathway to learning.

Mastering language is vital in team-based learning.

Most languages are full of color, variation, and rich diversity. English in particular is celebrated (or maligned, depending on your viewpoint) for its wide-ranging inclusion of synonyms, the vagaries of its idioms, and the frequent ambiguity of its words. The reason traces back to frequent cross-pollination of cultures as the Anglo-Saxons and Franks repeatedly invaded the native Celts, in what today is better known as Great Britain. It's a fascinating story with roots that trace to ancient Rome and Greece.

But two thousand years of semantic evolution creates modern day challenges when we seek to collaborate. The nuances of words and the intricacy of our language can prove challenging. There are, of course, some relatively easy ways to seek and achieve resolution if we're willing to make the effort. The history of words is a rich and accessible. Look at any dictionary (online or hard copy), or better still, a thesaurus. Count the definitions. Trace the synonyms. Take a moment to review the *etymology*, or origins of terms that prove confusing or ambiguous.

Of course, how we wield words can be a double-edged sword. If words are used to isolate or condescend to others, even if it's unintentional, we can quickly damage important relationships. Careless or even joking attempts to label or categorize individuals can drive a deep wedge in an otherwise healthy group dynamic. Words used to attack or criticize others routinely cripple the working dynamic of the group. So in our efforts to carefully name and categorize things, we must take care not to name or categorize our co-workers. It's rarely a case of the actual words being an issue, but rather, how our words are interpreted by the listener. In collaboration practice, our feelings about words often matter as much as the meaning of the words themselves.

Consider this scene, and sadly it's a common one. A team is working together on a problem, but it's locked in semantic debate. The group simply can't agree on key words being exchanged, and tempers have flared. Meaningful communication has all but ended even though the conversation continues. Several well-versed, impassioned stakeholders are going to the mat to defend their points, but with their terminology not defined they are talking in circles, going nowhere. What does the rest of the group do? Members can watch, take sides, or tune out completely. Again, quite sadly, these results are common. In such cases, collaboration essentially stops in its tracks.

Alternatively, we can dare to engage. We can identify the issue for what is it, and become catalysts for helping to define our most hotly contested terms. We don't have to be the ones to provide definitions. But we can be the ones to insist that definitions are required. In the process, we are driving a few important stakes in the ground. We're catalysts for consensus. We might even earn some respect.

When we find common terms, we build common ground.

Wittgenstein and George Lakoff shared an appreciation for the cultural implications of language that today we tend to take for granted. Language itself is created by a people as part of their culture. The origins and evolution of any language can be used to trace the historical advancement of the people who developed it. The value is to bring the deeply influential power of culture and language to our collaborative objectives and to master the semantics of language, rather than allowing the words—and those who wield them—to master us. Effective collaborators recognize the power of words and appreciate their implications. They invest time in choosing the right ones. When there are many words that could frame a solution, which ones are best aligned with the objective? Which phrases might best reflect the intent of the over-arching vision? What words would best communicate the desires of the collaborative team?

It comes down to appreciating the influential and inspirational power of words, and learning to wield them effectively—not as a weapon, but as a productive tool—with intent and precision. I can think of a few of my high school English teachers who would appreciate these sentiments. Let me offer a quick note of thanks for planting a few critical seeds.

Yes, I was paying attention.

TAKEAWAYS for "Semantics"

All of us are careless with our words now and then, but for some, this may an area worth a little intervention. We speak without thinking, letting our scattered, ill-defined notions fall where they may. Reflect on the main ideas from this chapter and decide the implications for yourself:

- **T1. To what extent are your learning & knowledge constrained by your vocabulary? Have you been at a loss for words and had it impact an important decision or meeting?**

- **T2. Do you tend to stick your foot in your mouth? What happens when you do?**

- **T3. Does rich & colorful language help us or hurt us when collaborating? When might semantic precision prove to be a better choice?**

- **T4. Have you ever used solution language in practice to build buy-in? Can you imagine a scenario when this approach might help you?**

- **T5. Like an iceberg, the implications of our words can hide beneath the surface of what's actually said. Is this to our advantage?**

These concepts flow directly into the next chapter, so answer carefully. We're assembling building blocks. Those forming the foundation—on the bottom tier—must be strong.

6 – Metaphor and Common Ground

Can We Relate?

If language is taken for granted in the modern world, then metaphor bears the same burden. After all, many say metaphor is one of the most powerful tools in the English language for conveying complex meaning. If we discount the value of words themselves, what hope does metaphor have?

Actually, we've already come across several examples of useful metaphors in the book, including:

M1. The Elements of Collaboration are like DNA
M2. Ideas are like leaves on a mountain stream
M3. Collaboration is puzzle solving
M4. Collaboration is like herding cats
M5. Ideas are like icebergs *(refer to FIGURE 12)*

Metaphors (and similes, the metaphor's more get-to-the-point sister construct using *like* or *as*) enhance understanding, by linking abstract concepts to something that's more concrete.

Note: I like to tag specific examples with a coded prefix—eg., M1, M2—for quick reference, making them easier to talk about when collaborating later. I'm going to shorten "metaphorical references" to metaphor for convenience, keeping in mind the grammatical rules I'll be dancing around a bit. For reference and comparison, you'll find a list of these provided in the back.

Strong metaphors change the game in collaboration. They connect the dots. They ground the diverse challenges of team interaction by using more visual, memorable, and real-world concepts. Metaphors help create a conceptual framework for a deep intuitive understanding of what's being discussed, grounded in our personal experience.[65] Everyone has played with blocks. We've all watched leaves in a river and solved puzzles. By now, most of us have tried herding a few cats— whether felines, children, or co-workers. Reflecting on references that generate vivid memories allows us to explore unique aspects of the subject matter in deeply intuitive ways.

A picture may be worth a thousand words, but a good metaphor can link that same visual element with a deeper meaning. Perhaps a good metaphor is worth two thousand words? It's not a rhetorical question, really. Think about it. The constructive and intentional use of a good metaphor fundamentally changes your ability to be understood, and it does so quickly. That's just short of magic in the collaboration process.

Metaphors change the game.

So where then do these metaphorical constructs come from? How can they be developed? I've found that coming up with a good metaphor can be a challenge, because their deep, intuitive nature means our brains must work overtime to come up with fairly intricate, logical connections. These connections tend to emerge from beneath our conscious thought processes. If you've had writer's block, you'll relate quickly to the challenges of metaphor development. It's at the core of creativity, which itself is an alchemist's process. So metaphor making doesn't lend itself to performing on demand. The harder we try to come up with a metaphor, the more rapidly our idea engine sputters. Perhaps ironically, when we're not focused directly on the problem, and often much later than we need it, the metaphor appears.

Dan Albergotti, reflecting on this cognitive alchemy, says that "metaphor only comes—if we're lucky—through the unconscious mind in an act of composition, when we've managed to outwit our consciousness with a pure focus on the senses. Metaphor is the truth of imagination, not the truth of the intellect."[66]

Imagine, for a moment, the all-too-common alternative: a world without metaphor. In the absence of these powerful semantic tools, we're left without easy ways to anchor abstractions, and much of the world seems to be a confusing jumble. We talk in circles. We shrug off discussion of difficult issues because we don't understand them. We fail to define important events and trends, completely at a loss to explain their implications, thus missing an opportunity for a useful exchange of ideas. We routinely relegate tough mental outcomes to chance. It's a world devoid of much deep thinking or knowledge gains, suffering from chronic loss of meaning, empty of any truly useful insights about the world and our stake in it, or a path for a viable future.

It's not exactly the kind of place we want to live.

But it sounds a bit like the 21st century.

As I've said already, we desperately need collaborative approaches to work ourselves out of this place. I argue that we'll need metaphor to get our biggest and best ideas communicated quickly. Sure, it takes a bit of work, and more than a little creative inspiration. But a good metaphor can serve as a surprisingly rapid means of getting to the point. It may be prove to be the shortest possible path to common ground. It helps us draw out similarities on a somewhat abstract or confusing topic—refining and refocusing different perspectives—in a concerted effort to make sense of things.

George Lakoff and Mark Johnson lead a fascinating review of all things metaphorical in *Metaphors We Live By* (1980). Some examples will illustrate the semantic power of the tool. I'll provide a few metaphors in a format Lakoff and Johnson used.[67] Some of these framings are familiar; others, less so. In every case, there are subtle implications to what's being conveyed. Think about each line. Watch how strong visual ideas, conveyed through language, help us understand how deeply images from our personal experience pervade and define (and are defined by) our culture. Notice how we wield these phrases as a means of getting a point across, with scarcely a thought.

M6. Time is Money.

How do you *spend* your time?

I've *invested* lots of energy in that project.

I can't *waste* any more time on that.

M7. Meetings are War.

He *defended* his point.

Her criticisms were *on target*.

My ideas were *shot down*.

Let's develop a *plan of attack*.

M8. Management is like a Railroad.

He was the *line manager* for my division.

His ideas were *derailed*.

Let's take that issue *off-line*.

I think that concept is taking us *off track*.

Was he able to *engineer* a solution?

Already we can see that metaphor, like the evolution of language, reflects a rich account of our history and our culture, often in subtle ways.

Consider the first metaphor listed: "M6 Time is Money"; the prominence of money and capital in our Western heritage is no secret, as finance has remained the backbone of the Industrial Revolution, and is deeply infused in our culture. Small wonder notions of time and money are embedded in our language. But do we realize how profoundly our culture reflects the battle grounds of our society, as is evident in: "M7 Meetings are War"? These references were more than likely fueled by memories of war, still fresh during the explosion of American business in the 1950's and 1960's. And who recalls from history books that transcontinental railroads in the 19th century created the first significant corporations that led to the formation of Wall Street? This influence seems to be clearly reflected in: "M8 Business Management is like a Railroad" [68] I see many fascinating nuances at work here. Thoughtful collaborators can drive rapid acceptance of their ideas by choosing metaphors that can illustrate the issues at hand.

Again, I conclude that collaboration on difficult problems can call for some heavy lifting. But let's examine a few simple metaphors that may help us unpack the collaboration challenge, using the same analytical structure we applied above. Here we'll focus on the flow and emergence of new ideas:

M2. Ideas are like leaves on a mountain stream.*
I can't *keep up* with that argument.
That concept is *getting away* from me.
The conversation *flowed too fast* to follow.
* from prior example, page 81

M9. Ideas are a tapestry.
I've lost the *thread* of his argument.
Let's work that into the *fabric* of the conversation.
I'm *torn* on how to proceed.

M10. Ideas are like a plant.
That idea is *growing* on me.
Her solution is *living proof* that we can achieve it.
We didn't solve it, but we *planted* important *seeds*.

When used together, related metaphors can create strong messages about the nature of the topic. In this case, our various notions of what constitutes ideas introduce a sense of flow (mountain stream), connection (threads in a tapestry) and growth (organic aspects).

Below the level of conscious reflection (as we introduced conceptually with the *Ideas are like Icebergs* metaphor, M5, FIGURE 12), understanding emerges. Relationships become evident and are retained, often at an emotional level. The concepts resonate, sometimes deeply.

With care and intent, metaphors work like magic.

You may notice some aspects of the particular "idea" metaphors above (M2, M9, M10), which, if taken together, serve to support and reinforce each other conceptually. Lakoff would say they are *coherent*. In the examples here, threads of a tapestry might flow into the loom that weaves the finished cloth. That same thread might be wound like a plant, or vine. Such connections among coherent metaphors can be especially valuable when trying to build collaborative common ground. On the other hand, metaphorical pairs may conflict, and their value rapidly falls off.

Lakoff cautions that few metaphors will align perfectly because, by their nature, they expose different aspects of the abstract subject at hand. The value is in comprehending each metaphor and learning from it. They should be employed when, where, and—it should be mentioned—only *if* they make sense. If a metaphor doesn't help to advance a situation, idea, or problem resolution, then we shouldn't continue using it. There is no value in forcing one. In fact, we lose ground and valuable time with the collaboration team if we repeatedly push a point that leads to a metaphorical dead end.

So what are some practical situations? Where might abstract subject matter warrant metaphors in action?

My years in the IT trenches have armed me with a trusted inventory of metaphors. I keep them close by at all times. IT concepts can seem very abstract so the space is chock full of them. They've become so prevalent that even my business-facing clients are comfortable using them as well. They seem to work independently of any specific industry or business problem, providing a sure sign that these particular metaphors are operating at full maturity:

M11. System Design is like a Building.
The platform was the *foundation* for further investments.
We discussed the viability of that *architecture*.
The solution *reinforced* our security posture.
The design gave us a good *frame* for discussion.

M12. Databases are like Containers.
Performance fell apart when the database grew beyond its specified *capacity*.
We called support; data had *overflowed* the cache.
The disk array created a *durable* back-up solution.

M13. IT Networks are like Plumbing.
He monitored the *flow* of user transactions.
The device was a *bottleneck*; data could no longer get through to the users.
I told the CFO we'd need to buy a bigger *pipe*.

Notions of buildings, containers, and plumbing are common ways we think about structure and flow in our world. Similar metaphors are at work in medicine, law, and across much of academia, including education and science. The late Richard Feynman, once a professor at Cornell and Cal Tech and a Nobel Prize-winning physicist in quantum mechanics, was well-known for using metaphors to describe the complex concepts of physics to his college students. Metaphor, it seems, is everywhere that abstract concepts call out to be deciphered.

Now let's look at how metaphor plays an increasing role in social system innovation and reform. Recall from our earlier chapters that our social systems, many of them "wicked problems," present perhaps the most complex challenges of all. Experts are everywhere, but they can scarcely agree on the problems, let alone solutions. In the context of public education, it's a storm of rich metaphorical dimensions.

First, we'll consider the powerful *factory metaphor,* which reflects the deep-seated, production-line workings of the Industrial Revolution. Factories produce goods in high volumes. Their managers focus on standardization to remove variance, with a high bias for controlling quality and costs. This model is highly effective for high-scale mass-production of goods like automobiles, but it doesn't work as well when applied to public education. Both Clayton Christensen and Sir Kenneth Robinson have voiced concerns by using this metaphor repeatedly in the last several years—with some success.[69] As you read the elements of this particular metaphor, pay attention to what resonates:

> **M14. Public Education is like a Factory**
> Do K12 curriculum *standards* ensure *compliance*?
> Can we *measure* student *performance* according to a *schedule*?
> Is *standardized testing* effective at reducing *defects*?
> Is the *system* working?

Educators often struggle with this metaphorical analysis because it seems to shortchange their commitment to teacher excellence. It seems to ignore the creativity being applied in some schools. And more generally, it turns a cold shoulder to the genuine care that so many teachers have for their students. Quite clearly, in this regard, the factory metaphor fails to describe a universal view. But remember Lakoff: every metaphor won't fit every perspective, but it's quite possible there's still intrinsic value. What if this metaphor can tell us something else? As it happens, this particular metaphor does, in fact, resonate with many K12 issues that derive from scale. How can we provide public education to tens of millions of children in a highly consistent, standardized manner? We treat it like a factory. The batches (class sizes) get larger and larger, variance becomes the enemy, and we end up with what we have in K12 Education today.

Now let's consider an alternative metaphor for public education. This one has emerged in the K12 ecosystem in the past few years to describe a different way to learn. In formal research it is called *connectivism,* but the more common name for it is *rhizomatic learning.* The concept links the learning process to the growing habits of rhizomes, like potatoes and irises—plants with deep, resilient root systems.[70]

M15. Learning is like a Rhizome.
The student explored *multiple paths* to the answer.
The hands-on learning experience proved *resilient.*
The curriculum was *grounded* in practical application.
Her approach had *deep roots* in project-based methods.

Suddenly, to me, the factory looks like a dark place for learning, and the view from the vegetable garden takes on new dimensions.

These metaphors and others like them can spark profound insights among deeply invested practitioners. In this case it's teachers and administrators and the ecosystem's many stakeholders, including parents, students and even legislators.

So we can see that metaphors can influence people, literally capturing their imaginations, helping them grapple with ideas and concepts that are foreign to their mental models, and challenging the paradigms of their own experience. If reinforced and nurtured, they serve to create new insight and more common ground. Well-crafted metaphors can accelerate a collaborative effort.

How can we apply metaphor to our problem-solving efforts in a practical way? Steven Johnson's, *Where Good Ideas Come From,* is literally packed with useful metaphorical references. In fact, Johnson challenges us to build on three adaptive structures that have come about in our world—the coral reef, the city, and the Internet—that represent very interesting examples of *emergence* at work.[71] In these places we see growth, creativity, and resilience. In these places, like no other, our ecosystems have flourished. Can these examples of emergence in our world provide a metaphorical breeding ground for collaborators?

Review these metaphorical constructs, in the context of collaboration:

M16. Collaboration is like a Coral Reef.

New ideas *emerged* from our original insights.
The new concept is *built upon* our past thinking.
His insights were *supported* by historical facts.

M17. Collaboration is like a City.

The framework is *central* to our solution design.
It may be more efficient to *consolidate* our insights according to function.
We avoided the *traffic jam* by directing concerns down an *alternate route*.

M18. Collaborating is like Using the Internet.

Our session was led by a *network* of practitioners.[72]
We need to *search* for some common ground.
Can we *connect* with a few key experts on this?

In practice, it's about coming up with a metaphor that seems to work, giving some examples, and creating useful linkages that lead to understanding. New ideas come alive. As we collaborate with metaphors at our command, we create new, informative, real-world relevance. A simple subset of the same words, by themselves, might leave us confused or disoriented. Metaphors open new doors.

TAKEAWAYS for "Metaphor"

Mastering metaphors will provide a significant advantage to anyone seeking to drive understanding on abstract topics. Collaborators face this at every turn. How can we best be prepared to use these constructs?

- **T1. From Aristotle to Lakoff, much has been said re: the power of metaphor to make the abstract more clear; what are your favorite examples?**

- **T2. How does the factory metaphor for learning (re: defects) stack up against a more organic metaphor, like the rhizome (re: rooted resilience) from your personal experience? What do you see as the more productive learning environment?**

- **T3. Steven Johnson's Reef, City & Web metaphors help us see how emergence happens in our everyday world. What other examples can you think of? Something based on weaver/ grower perhaps?**

If a metaphor is truly worth two thousand words, then it's possible our narratives and short stories are about to get shorter. Let's investigate that. Story is our next topic.

7 – Storytelling

Connecting Actions and Outcomes

By now, you can see how the building blocks of Collaboration DNA are being stacked, one-by-one. On top of language, we placed metaphor. On top of metaphor, we'll now place *story*.

Early in our lives, we hear stories told by parents and come to depend on them for learning; but like metaphor, it's easy to take the power of stories for granted. Story is a deep means of communicating big ideas over time. Scriptures from every faith are consistent in developing strong, intuitive, and emotional vignettes for conveying meaning. It's truly an ancient form, a way of communicating deeply that is embedded in every culture, and is a central cultural force that influences how we conceptualize and remember abstract ideas, values, and morals.[73]

Unfortunately, it's a skill that not everyone fully develops. And that's a problem for collaborators.

We've been raising the bar, so let's not stop now.

Story goes beyond the simple communication of needs or ideas. A good story is comprised of principles, not fixed rules. Story fosters the development of timeless human archetypes (reflecting the deep human essence), not lifeless stereotypes (projecting an inhuman shell). It's part of our discovery, helping us to recognize patterns and inner truths, helping us make sense of the world around us.[74]

With our emphasis on semantic language and metaphor to fuel improved collaboration, effective storytelling essentially allows us to deliver on those deeper investments. The literary elements work together, creating scaffolding that brings structure in two areas: how we think, and how we get our ideas across to others. It's difficult to imagine effective collaboration that doesn't bring the unified use of these elements into play.

Dan Pink lists story as one of the six competencies of a right-brain directed future, as he cites Mark Turner: "Stories are easier to remember, because stories are how we remember … most of our experience, knowledge, and thinking is organized as stories."[75] Good stories are "facts put into context, enriched by emotion … [and] they almost always pack an emotional punch."[76]

As with language in general, and metaphor more specifically, the frequency, depth, and quality of our reading investments builds our mastery with words. Our improved command of language nourishes our ability to learn and inquire. Our imagination expands. Like a rhizome our ability to collaborate establishes deep roots. The additional practice gained by wielding these communication forms through written and verbal collaboration can only improve our ability to engage in increasingly valuable ways.

Story is often the space where our new ideas take shape.

We'll discuss the notion of space later, but for now, think of story—and its commercial cousin, the *narrative*—as containers for our emerging ideas. Reading or hearing a well-crafted passage helps us acquire the full meaning, intention, emotional import, and moral content of a message. As listeners, starting from our earliest childhood, we've come to value the deep learning that often comes with a good story.

But then it's our turn to communicate. Suddenly we must face the opposite direction, and be creative. When we need to come up with a story in the collaboration context, the responsibility now falls upon us. Thought leaders, consultants, change agents, marketers and politicians understand the power of story (and metaphor) in leading change. Collaborators must learn from them, and leverage their techniques. Mull over your favorite storytellers of all time, or go back to the classics. As you reread them, watch not only for the impact the story has on you as a reader, but watch also for techniques that capture your attention.

What did you learn?

How did you feel?

In what ways did the storyteller inspire your interest or foster your enthusiasm? [77]

If we think about the implications, our idea of collaboration can take on new, more interesting dimensions. We can begin to set aside the drudgery of arguments defended by facts and figures, or appeals to personality, political loyalties or past favors. Story unlocks energy and empathy in all of us, and has been doing so since ancient tribes could communicate.

Storytelling is about communicating a message in powerfully relevant ways, appealing to the listener's shared sentiments and values, using a language they can understand. Metaphor is not absolutely required for a good story, but it clearly enables the communication of big ideas, engaging the reader/listener at the deepest possible level—where true understanding and buy-in are the dominant forces. A good story transcends communication, and becomes a significant source of education and inspiration.

A story doesn't have to follow the strict genre rules of course, with a developed set of characters, a plot, and a climax. A short vignette or narrative passage can deliver all the value of a good story in a smaller, lighter-weight package. In business and collaborative settings, being succinct can only help us. We've touched on the breakneck pace of our 21st century world, fueled by always-on access to information and content that's served up to us via the web and countless cable and satellite channels. The demand for our attention is relentless.

In many ways, our short stories can't be short enough.

A great venue emerging from social media is the increasingly commonplace blog platform. Hosted here are incredibly concise snippets of insight, whether reaching us as narratives, vignettes or very short stories. Blogs provide us with a virtual scratchpad to share our thoughts. And, while bloggers can keep typing and posting for days on end, the typical blogger writes in chunks of around 500 words, pausing to take a breath every few days, so we might digest the input before the next round of ideas springs forth. But perhaps the most powerful feature of a blog is the ability to accept and respond to reader comments. Our ideas evolve from the strength of inputs and insights of others. In fact, many of the core ideas in this book—including all the research on culture and critical thinking—started out as blog posts, before I had come upon a full notion of Collaboration DNA. To me, that's creative emergence in action. An insight appears. There is positive feedback. The thinking turns into a small research project, which grows into a bigger, more comprehensive one. The outline of a book takes shape. Don't look now, but you are holding it in your hands.

Such is the intrinsic power of a narrative story. We plant seeds, and they start to grow.

One of my favorite blog posts is "Koan Zero" by Steve Barth.[78] It's a very short narrative with a premise that is blindingly simple, based on a metaphorical construct: *"Knowledge Sharing is like breathing in and out."*

If only collaboration were so easy.

As I said at the outset, the power and will to collaborate is a decision that's up to each and every one of us. Is collaboration important? You decide how to finish the story.

TAKEAWAYS for "Story"

How might we apply storytelling in our collaborative efforts? It may be easier than you think. Here are some specific areas where awareness of the art and craft of storytelling can drive collaborative engagement to a much richer place, putting some of the classic elements of story writing into our collaborative, problem solving context.

- **T1. Essential Questions. What's the big idea of our story? What are we trying to accomplish?**

- **T2. Conflict and Challenges. Good stories introduce and resolve a conflict that impacts the future, e.g., success vs. failure, gain vs. loss. Can you frame your narrative along these lines can help drive a point home more vigorously?**

- **T3.Stakeholders. Who are the players in our problem/solution stories and how might we connect with them?**

- **T4. Change Events. As stakeholders face challenges and conflicts in your story, what situations drive meaningful outcomes? Try linking outcomes to your collaborative intent, the goal or problem frame.**

- **T5. Engagement. How do we ensure a connection with our listeners, so that our narrative resonates with their own personal experiences?**

Each of these areas represents a significant aspect in the craft of story and the art of storytelling. Master these elements, and watch your team's collaborative connections grow deeper.

PART 3: RELATIONSHIPS

"Our range of creative expression increases when we join with others. New relationships create new capacities."

Margaret Wheatley

8 – Are We Listening?

Learning to Engage

Collaboration starts with our ability to listen. That's also where it often stops. As a society, we don't listen well, and we haven't been listening for quite some time.

It's not just about hearing what has been said. To drive engagement, a fundamentally deeper level of connection is required. The human mind tends to race and it impacts our ability to communicate. Collaboration requires that we learn to suspend the inner voice in our heads that never seems to stop talking. It's hard work. But focus and conscious effort are critical.

Listening wasn't always my strong suit. As a male, I've long admitted to being "Y-chromosome impaired" but I've only recently come to appreciate the implications. I've read much on the psychology of relationships, including books by Daniel Goleman (author of *Emotional Intelligence*, and more recently *Social Intelligence*) and John Gray (the man behind *Men are from Mars, Women are From Venus*). From their pages flowed the sobering news: there's scarcely any skill more precious for humans—and men in particular—than learning how to listen.

Today's breakneck world is full of distractions. Our smart phones seem to vie for every second of our attention. We scarcely have time for broader topics, routinely skipping over anything that passes for deep reflection. And if we *do* manage to focus for a short while, our ability to retain what we've learned presents yet another set of hurdles.

Effective communication is increasingly against the odds.

So it's apparent: collaboration requires that we attack active listening directly.

How do we do that?

The biggest problem after lack of awareness is that we don't take the time to develop the skills. Learning to communicate more effectively is, for most of us, a mundane personal improvement item, right next to being organized, minding your manners, and doing your homework. It's far too easy to assume the mention of improved communication is sufficient, giving it lip-service and checking off the box. From my experience, a great many people attempting to collaborate are actually poor communicators. It's an issue that's generally independent of their intellect, management talent, or even other social skills.

Unfortunately, active listening is not something we can postpone until later. It's on our critical path.

We must be active listeners out of the gate.

It must start with being present.

To bring this point home, it's worth discussing the dynamics in more detail. What happens when people come together? For starters, verbal and non-verbal cues are exchanged quickly. Greetings are offered. There are gestures, and generally hand-shakes. People move toward or away from each other in a dance that is at once inquiry and negotiation. As this unfolds, most will subconsciously assess their ability to relate to and communicate with each other, especially in a collaborative setting where information exchange is at a premium. Is this new person a friend, or a foe? Will I be able to get along with them? Do I want them sitting next to me, or as far away from me as possible?

If you're checked out or distracted early on, others will notice it, and they may lose confidence in you as a participant. Groups can be highly sensitive to productivity and impatient with wasting time. There may be few opportunities to say "let me try that one on you a different way" or "hey John, are you listening?" Collaborators need to bring their "A" game, striving for that elusive 100%.

FIGURE 13 shows some characteristic factors that influence our ability to engage. I've seen all of these prove important during collaboration, focusing our listening and helping us connect in meaningful ways with others:

Factors that Influence Engagement		Why Are They Important?
1	Bias for Respect	The level of respect among a group can be difficult to gauge. Are healthy boundaries in place? Does everyone value input from others? Can members subordinate their own views and opinions?
2	Bias for Trust	Building trust takes time and for collaborating teams there's not a moment to lose. Are we willing to engage? Do we trust the team enough to take risks?
3	Active-Listening	When we're planning our next comment, true listening is difficult.
4	Empathy	This is an important social skill that derives from our ability to sense emotion in others.
5	Positive Outlook	Positive energy helps generate esprit de corps and a productive learning environment.
6	Goal Orientation	Focusing on discrete outcomes is a good motivator to pay more attention. Are we thinking about our ultimate intention, and bringing a healthy mindset to the table?

FIGURE 13 – Factors influencing Group Engagement
Looking at observable behaviors that make a difference

Behaviors and skills like the ones here can be readily observed and group leaders should pay attention to them. Quite simply, the level of engagement among team members is one of the first early warning signals a collaborative group will demonstrate. The willingness and ability for group members to listen to each other is a critical data point.

What can we learn?

When most or all of the team members are strong in the areas summarized by FIGURE 13, deep and active listening can occur and the level of communication begins to build, sometimes quite rapidly. The opportunity for effective collaboration is unlocked.

But what happens when one or more team members are *not* strong in these areas? Based on statistics alone, won't every group have outliers and hold-outs?

Sadly, yes, there will be detractors. And collaboration will break down rapidly in these circumstances, if it ever gets off the ground in the first place. From my experience, getting past this can be difficult. We're more than likely not acting on behalf of the HR department, and to a point, it's not our job to counsel others on how they should act when they come to work. Many collaborative efforts fail outright at this stage. The advocates of collaboration give up in the face of negative dynamics.

But we're not dead in the water. There are ways to push through this. It takes strong leadership and interpersonal skills, and some faith that individuals can adapt. I'm a strong believer that groups can own their own behavioral standards, defining what everyone in that local setting believes is acceptable. Yes, organizational culture enters into this, which we'll discuss in Chapter 10. But there's hope.

We can isolate and improve conditions locally.

Effective groups will rally in the face of negative energy, asking members to raise expectations across the team, challenging each person to sustain collaboration goals. Such groups negotiate ground rules. They insist on fostering the ability to listen among its members. They share. They focus on building trust and respect, and talk about it openly. They work out differences quickly online (real-time) or offline, if necessary. They focus on building momentum, getting into the collective zone of collaboration. When this works the resonance is literally palpable, and it is reflected in the results.

I know it's possible, because I've personally experienced it. Here's the story:

Memories of Qualex OSP
Insights on Listening

I've served on many teams and played many roles in 30 years of business, but my personal high-water mark for collaboration stands out clearly. It was at Qualex, a subsidiary of Eastman Kodak based in Durham, NC. At the time, Qualex was well known as an industry leader in photographic film processing.

I'd come in as IT Director for the On-Site Processing (or "OSP") division, a fast growth unit that had spun out from the core Qualex overnight business. For 7 years I was a member of the OSP Leadership Team, ultimately reporting to George Briggs, our divisional executive. During his tenure, he built on a tradition of strong leaders who listened, empowering our various functional teams to take ownership, counting on us to make good decisions to support our major retail customers.

These dynamics created a collaborative working environment that allowed us to flourish. As the division continued to grow, I worked side-by-side with colleagues in operations, finance, and accounting. We organized an IT steering group and built plans to implement a stand-alone, cost-effective infrastructure geared for growth. We pulled ideas from our diverse backgrounds or created new ones, ultimately finding consensus on those that seemed most viable.

Our collaboration proved successful. We created a thriving retail sales and service operation. In a few short years, we'd gone from a skeleton crew running on a spreadsheet to a significant business with a full-service call center supporting 13,000 one-hour photo minilabs nationwide.

We accomplished much in a short time.

Looking back now, the most amazing thing to me was that we stayed united in purpose and approach for the duration of our time together, a period of almost seven years. There were challenges along the way, to be sure. But over those years, those colleagues—who were also my internal customers—became good friends.

It's been a decade since that team disbanded, though some in the group still get together to look back and smile. Such is the legacy of collaboration. Deeper levels of engagement are possible when team members truly listen. Strong relationships form. And diverse stakeholders facing unique demands can function as a seamless whole. I think I learned more about business in those seven years than I have in my other 23. I certainly learned a great deal about collaboration. Only the relentless advance of technology, in our case, digital photography, could unwind what we had built.

Once you've experienced such an open and productive working environment, it can be frustrating later not to have it when you need it. For me, the silver lining may be the internal standard that emerges, the "personal best" that can serve as a guide post for what's possible.

What about structure in our communication, and the idea of goals? Do we really need it? Doesn't it constrain creativity?

We'll explore balanced objectives in Part 4, but I remain convinced that a bit of structure helps create focus and keeps goals in view, especially early in the game. Communication in groups can be chaotic when there's a lack of structure. When individuals resist goals or objectives—or when they can't work to find common ground—the collaborative productivity of the group will drop off rapidly.

In open-ended scenarios, topics change frequently, sometimes even in real time. This can cause teams to lose valuable time and momentum. Group members become reactive. Conversely, if everyone knows what they're trying to accomplish, they'll know better what precisely to listen *for*. The group must be willing and able to sustain focus for collaboration to produce results. Groups can attempt to collaborate without goals, but will generally accomplish little. Those *with* goals have a working sense of the purpose at hand, allowing the sustained focus necessary to achieve breakthroughs.[79]

Healthy group dynamics are a function of what individuals bring in terms of experience or depth in the six areas outlined in FIGURE 13. If there are deficiencies, gaps, or hurdles, sometimes a strong leader can create some short-term momentum through brute force facilitation, taking a more directive role. It's an uphill battle, and there are no guarantees, and it's an approach that works against desired team dynamics. The better scenario calls for everyone to work from a position of strength, essentially sharing the load, and helping to drive toward a collective buy-in. This was my experience at Qualex.

In a commercial setting, I believe that objective criteria like those found in FIGURE 13 can make excellent screening criteria for the formation of new collaborative work groups. Leaders can nominate candidates based on their collaborative potential, and those demonstrating these traits can and should see their selection as a reward from management. After all, not everyone can bring these skills and traits to the table; those who can bring talents that will serve them well as collaborators, and thus deserve recognition. We'll need motivators like this downstream, when it's time to address culture change. The ability to engage with others matters deeply. It's worth focus and reflection, and any amount of proactive intervention that can be achieved.

So what if others still aren't playing ball after you've appealed?

Stay tuned for Chapters 9 through 12, where we'll look at additional steps for building healthy relationships and stronger teams, helping to foster organizations that are fundamentally better connected.

Sometimes, after all, we need a Plan B.

TAKEAWAYS for "Listening"

Beyond those personal attributes from FIGURE 13, there are additional approaches that anyone can learn to become a better listener. Here are some that I've found helpful:

- **T1. Stop talking and stop judging. Be fully "in the moment"—try hanging onto every word of the speaker, or at least, most of them.**

- **T2. Make frequent eye contact with the speaker. Don't stare, of course, but make it clear that you are listening and paying attention.**

- **T3. Ask questions. Advance the conversation and clarify key points.**

- **T4. Never allow yourself to talk over others (no matter how enthusiastic you are!) and discourage that behavior among team members—if there's still too much cross-talk happening, create a "virtual baton" denoting whose turn it is to talk, and pass it around the table.**

- **T5. Take notes.**

- **T6. Set An Example. In cases where there are individual-level behaviors that keep people from listening or becoming engaged, setting group standards and appealing to the needs**

of the group is important—sometimes this will sway or convert them.

Actively following these steps is almost certain to optimize your engagement in collaborative settings. And practice helps considerably.

9 – Hijacked

Heuristics, Instincts and Fear

Passion and intrigue are the stuff of songwriters and poets, to be certain. The ultimate reasons humans do what we do often remains a mystery. From a more scientific perspective, psychologists tell us that our emotions are deeply rooted in our animal nature, driving our behaviors when we feel our survival or our stake in the world may be impacted.[80] Logic often leaves us when our emotions enter in, and our ability to anticipate our specific actions tends to falter.

With emotions in charge, our actions seem unpredictable.

To me, it's a fascinating part of the collaboration story. If nothing else, this insight can help us see why emotion is seen as the enemy of precision and certainty in the Industrial World, a place where inconsistent performance due to human emotions has long taken a backseat to logic, quality standards, defect avoidance, and the careful accumulation of cold, hard facts. But what does all this mean to collaborators?

We're going to need to explore the notion of instincts and emotional triggers quite a bit further, because we'll soon see that these factors can impact our ability to collaborate. Through advances in neuroscience and modern psychology, we're learning more and more about how the human brain triggers alternative, unanticipated responses in certain situations.

The story takes some very interesting turns.

At some point in our lives we're advised to trust our instincts, and it's a notion backed-up by human history. Modern man has survived many millennia by learning what it takes to outwit our environment and our natural enemies. Our instincts act like an early warning system, increasing our chances of being around another day. Stepping off city curbs and approaching a cliff's precipice give us pause for good reason, and it's our instincts, housed in the brain's *amygdala*, that deserve the credit.[81]

Instinctive reactions will trigger when we sense danger, but also when we encounter situational patterns that we've seen in the past. Buying a car comes to mind, or perhaps, deciding on a mate. In nonlife-threatening situations such as these, instinct still plays a role, but the predefined social and emotional solutions are suddenly less clear-cut. In the more mundane, nonlife-threatening, workaday sense, instincts seem to play a role, but their life-saving precision begins to falter. Without facts or exact solutions at our disposal, we start looking at more general patterns to see what's worked for us before. I see it as the middle space between high-order logic and raw animal instinct.

We're entering the domain of *heuristics,* a generic set of solutions that our brains can use to solve problems in emergencies, or when our facts and logic fail us. We'll look at some examples just ahead.

Psychologists are still researching these dynamics and many questions remain[82] but there is increasing evidence from *fMRI* technology to indicate that our brains are indeed firing to solve problems from the deepest regions where our emotions and instinct reside.

Our brains are busy places. Much is happening beneath the surface of our thoughts. In certain situations, including ones we're about to explore, we act instinctively based on a view that our subconscious mind has of the world, without ever knowing for certain why.[83] Generally speaking, this does no harm. But when we're trying to collaborate, is it possible that our conditioned brain, geared for survival, *perceives* an emergency that isn't really there? Is it not possible for fear to trigger panic and flood our thoughts with an emotional response?

This is a pattern that I see taking shape in the field again and again. As we try to collaborate, many at the table are pushing away.

One theory is that our survival instincts are firing and making us defensive at just the wrong moment, when the problem at hand calls for more rational, reflective critical thinking.[84] Here's the psychological rationale: we know that emotional responses trigger when we feel threatened, or under attack, even when there is no legitimate basis. They trigger when we feel vulnerable. These responses can even trigger when we're feeling overwhelmed, tired, or out of control.[85] Psychologists believe such reactions completely undermine our ability to engage in critical thinking. It's a process that's called *hi-jacking*, which we'll come back to in Chapter 11. Heuristics can hurt us when this happens, sending us on a detour from more rational thought, essentially bypassing our high-end cognitive powerhouse, the *PFC*, or pre-frontal cortex, the part of our brains where we make decisions based on logic. If it's not an emergency, the PFC uses logic to decide what we should do.

What happens when our emotions enter the equation? Instinctive reactions will fire when we sense danger, which can include strong emotional stimuli to external events, including a sense of panic. Our instincts can save lives, but they can also lead us into trouble if they fire when they perceive an emergency that may not be there. If our brains need a quick answer, or if the facts aren't stacking up for us in a logical, productive way, our brains offer up a heuristic in response.

There's a certain degree of risk when we collaborate, because we become vulnerable. Our lack of knowledge is there for all to see. So of all emotions that impact us day to day, I believe there is only one that is predominant in the collaborative dynamic: and that's *fear*.

Fear is the emotion that our emergency response system uses to ensure our survival. In the social, organizational and commercial contexts that wrap around our notion of career and financial livelihood, this is not a trivial statement. Fear of survival and its close cousin, fear of failure, are deeply embedded in the psyche of our business culture and our society as a whole.

So what might happen if the pressures arising from a collaboration scenario were to suddenly overwhelm us? What could trigger if attempts to collaborate presented us with too many decision points that were too demanding, too risky, or simply too much to process? Given our neural wiring and social conditioning for survival, the answer to me is increasingly clear: our emergency systems would tell us to disengage, to step away from the information cliff, and to avoid the collaboration curb at all costs.

The emotion of fear may prove to be a profound barrier for many in their willingness to collaborate.

As I've watched collaborations succeed and fail, I've begun to see patterns in this area. Fear of survival is a strong motivator in organizational settings, whereas it's generally absent in the public domain. On the web, collaborators are often able to exchange insight at face value, with little fear of consequence or reprisal. They operate from a position of independent thought leadership and an open desire to learn more. I've seen it in numerous Twitter chats and blog posts, and I know that it's possible.

To me, that's telling.

Information overload alone can have similar effects on us. From a content perspective, we've discussed how the 21st Century can be massively over-stimulating, flooding us with information. At times it can seem a bit intimidating. Add to that proliferation of choices: hundreds of cable channels, hundreds upon hundreds of choices at dozens of local retail stores, and more gaming technologies than we can shake our controllers at. Proliferation in our consumer economy has run its course. It's almost too much for us to cope with.

I think we've begun, *instinctively*, to tune it out.

And the reaction many have to social media may be very much related: more information than can be realistically processed.

Given our fear of overload, I believe that the emergency neurons in our brains are starting to fire more and more often, triggering instinctive survival responses. Look around. Look at your co-workers. Look in the mirror. Do people you know seem impulsive, impatient, withdrawn, or depressed? Do you see people acting in ways that defy the common sense of logic?

Do you see smart people acting irrationally?

Performance demands up the ante, of course. As we climb the corporate ladder, the price of mistakes grows rapidly. Because we're increasingly afraid to make mistakes, we instinctively disengage more and more often, avoiding every cliff and every curb. We play it safe. We don't think twice about the consequences, and I'd argue we don't even think once. Margaret Wheatley sums up it up well, explaining our collective, culturally-influenced frame mind:

> *"Extinction will follow swiftly on the heels of any mistake. Creativity ceases. Fear of error seems to be the darkest of Darwinian shadows."*[86]

I believe fear for survival and fear of failure routinely strike death-blows to collaboration in most organizations.

But this is just the tip of our metaphorical iceberg, M5.

As our modern world floods us with additional information, the early warning systems that Goleman describes as "low-road" or "rapid response" brain functions are apt to trigger more and more often in our personal lives as well.

Everything seems to be about survival, so our instincts react accordingly. We tend to engage less and less. By default, our willingness to take risks is ever more rapidly hi-jacked by an early warning system that is hard-wired for safety. This isn't all bad, of course, but if this is our primary mode of operating, our willingness to take any risks is severely compromised. And we can't forget:

Collaboration and learning require that we take risks.

I believe we can point to the hair trigger reactions of our brain's emergency response system for more than a few detours on the path to collaboration. What are the perceived emergencies? I see several:

1. **Insecurity about our lack of knowledge**
2. **Not keeping up with or understanding a conversation**
3. **Not knowing an answer**
4. **Not having a good question**
5. **Rejection by colleagues or superiors**
6. **Failed performance, leading to job loss**

We might call these: "The Top Six Fears of Collaborators." In a healthy, positive learning environment, we'd find none of these concerns because *a truly collaborative environment values curiosity, risk-taking, and critical thinking*. The negative situations above, by definition, do not exist in a culture than advocates learning and knowledge sharing. In such organizations, we are not there to show what we know, but to increase what we know, which of course echoes the classic fixed vs. growth mindset we've discussed in Chapter 4, as outlined by Carol Dweck.[87]

When discussing empathy in Chapter 8, we touched on a powerful emotional programming process by which our brains learn to respond to situations—whether positive or negative—based on past experience. When this youthful learning is accompanied by any sort of trauma, the programmed experiences can be deep and powerful, literally burned-in to the psyche of the individual.

In FIGURE 14, I'll recap several important examples of mental heuristics, triggers that force a rapid answer without allowing the thinking brain to engage further. For each mental heuristic shown, imagine what might happen during collaboration if one or more participants allowed their instinctive reactions to take over. Could the quality of our deeper, analytical, more critical discussions be affected? Of course in true emergency situations we are far better off honoring them, than waiting to second guess them.[88] It's the pseudo-emergencies triggered by emotions like fear and panic that we need to be challenge.

	Mental Heuristic	Negative Implications	Positive Implications
1	Status quo	INERTIA associated with lower risk "Why change?"	Precedent – it has worked before
2	Hoarding Minimize effort & conserve calories	INERTIA associated with preserving resources – "I'm not going to waste my precious time on this."	Survival – stockpiling of resources is sometimes necessary
3	Mimicry Go along with the group	INERTIA through following the lead of a crowd – "Let's just go with the flow."	Resonance – in certain situations, mimicry can accelerate consensus and synthesis
4	Stereotype	Jumping to Conclusions – making snap judgments too quickly	-
5	Negativity	Non-productive Worry – unnecessary loss of focus, energy; can be disruptive	-
6	Simplicity	Risk of over-simplifying – eliminating critical variables	"Keep it Simple" – can help us identify solutions to complex problems
7	Foraging	-	Discovery – actively seeking new insight

FIGURE 14 – Mental Heuristics influencing Collaboration
Adapted from W. Herbert (2010)

Do you see a trend here? It's inertia of course. It's a common, default tendency to pull away, resisting engagement, and deferring to others. In the silo-thinking organization it's an epidemic, something we've known all along. It's the portrait of organizational bureaucracy.

I am hopeful with this new clarity we can at last come to terms with the problem, and begin to organize our energies around fixing it. We must learn to think and reflect in the moment, guarding against quick, instinctive, defensive, survival-oriented reactions. Our first step is to become aware of what is happening. Critical thinking needs to stay in the mix.

TAKEAWAYS for "Heuristics"

The most significant challenge is detecting mental heuristics in action because, by definition, they operate below our level of conscious awareness. Detecting them is going to be difficult. Here are some ideas to attempt breakthroughs:

- **T1. Keep the "Top Six Fears of Collaborators" top of mind. Review the list. Keep it with you. In the next group situation where you feel anxious or distracted, challenge yourself: can you correlate your emotional discomfort with any of these factors? Are these concerns real, or in your mind?**

- **T2. Review the "Inventory of Mental Heuristics that Impact Collaboration" in FIGURE 14—attempt the same exercise: when feeling anxious in a group, is it possible you are jumping to a heuristic, ignoring your rational capacity to analyze the facts and come to a logical conclusion?**

- **T3. Work on Differentiation—in FIGURE 14, three heuristics will likely prove to be the most difficult to discern, because they operate on a "value continuum" ranging from negative impact to positive. Remember, not all heuristics are bad. Can you tell which ones straddle the value continuum? The answer key is in the back.[89] Try jotting down factors that would help you determine whether a situation that invokes one of these 3 heuristics would end up being positive or negative forces. What would you do if the factors were inconclusive?**

When we seek to change our behavior, awareness is always the very first hurdle we must overcome. Invest time at this stage if you seek to be less captive to automatic responses that short circuit your thinking self.

There is no right or wrong behavior here; we are discussing the body's psychological response to its environment, over the course of a lifetime. Depending on how your personal mental circuits are wired, your skill as a collaborator may be fundamentally improved with focus in this area.

10 – The Dilemma of Culture

When we're talking about the problems across our organizations, it's easy to drop the notion of *culture* into the mix with little reflection. It's a powerful word that unifies our collective frustrations. It's a vague but strangely reassuring reference to social forces or norms that influence our behavior. It calls to mind far-off places where rules are established and decisions made with an uncanny effect on our day-to-day lives, while offering no court of appeal. We seem to know whether a culture is good, bad, or something in between, yet there's no script for creating one and serious doubt among academics and practitioners as to whether it can be intentionally changed.[90]

I've found culture is all of these things.

Part of why it's easy to blame culture for our troubles is that there are no specific individuals on the receiving end. Like the "system" or the "establishment" in past eras, we can lay our grievances at the doorstop of culture and feel fully justified, if not relieved, for having done so.

I was intrigued in 2009 when the problem of culture kept coming up in conversations on social media and its sluggish adoption by the mainstream. At the time, my understanding of the topic was shallow and uninformed. I did a little digging, and started connecting the dots. What I learned began to explain much about why our best efforts to achieve change come up short.[91] When it comes to collaboration, culture provides a backdrop that brings powerful forces to bear on how we allow ourselves to think. Ultimately, it informs our approach to interpersonal relationships.

Let's look at some examples. Do we tend to trust each other? Do we tend to share information? Do we tend to respect the boundaries and priorities of others? Of course our answers will vary in specific relationships, but an organizational culture sets the tone, creating the default scenario for that specific environment. Go to the organization across the street and the answers to these questions will be different.

Culture is the foundation of behavioral norms within a specific group. It's an accumulation of how our predecessors have viewed success historically. It's useful to note that culture is bi-directional: it both shapes and is shaped by its members. Peter Drucker called culture "amorphous" (without form) because of the many variables influencing it and the difficulty in predicting its outcomes.[92]

Like mental heuristics, organizational culture isn't all good or bad but represents the cumulative sense of an organization's view. It functions in layers, with multiple influences interacting. Cultural forces of ethnicity, nationality, family, religion, functional or domain expertise, and even academic affiliation combine in unique ways to influence how people believe they should behave. Add to that mix an organization's particular culture and it is little wonder the average person struggles to establish realistic expectations for themselves and for others. Each layer represents an integral part of the expectations scheme, but it can be difficult to unwind or analyze specific cultural influences. In extreme situations, in the words of Bill Eggers, a kind of organizational schizophrenia sets up, due to cultural alignment problems that are structural, fueling perpetual conflict and inefficiencies; his case study: the U.S. Federal Government.[93]

What specific cultural rules guide our behavior when we seek to collaborate? That's difficult to answer, because it will depend on the situation and on which cultural forces are in play for the individual. But there are, in fact, some important and interesting patterns that can help shed some light.

When it comes to collaboration, prevailing cultural forces can work in both directions—either in favor of sharing knowledge, or in the opposite direction, tending to maintain a bias for control. That's why, in our Western society, I've come to believe organizational culture serves as a barrier more often than not. It doesn't need to be that way, of course, nor is it a desirable state of affairs. Yet cultures with silos that resist change and seek to control seem to prevail in most organizations. To understand why this is the case, let's look at four established cultural patterns within modern organizations—each of them quite common—based on the work of the respected Organizational Development thought leader, Charles Handy.[94]

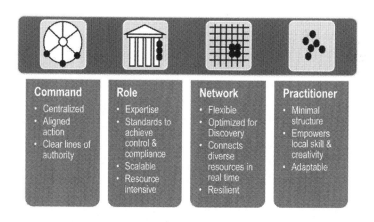

Command	Role	Network	Practitioner
• Centralized	• Expertise	• Flexible	• Minimal structure
• Aligned action	• Standards to achieve control & compliance	• Optimized for Discovery	• Empowers local skill & creativity
• Clear lines of authority	• Scalable	• Connects diverse resources in real time	• Adaptable
	• Resource intensive	• Resilient	

FIGURE 15 – Four Types of Organizational Culture
Assessment of implications; adapted from C. Handy (1993)

These four models are summarized in FIGURE 15. Large, complex interconnected enterprises, like a modern hospital or a military unit, will have many of these subcultures clearly visible, working in tandem. As you examine the diagram, see if you can identify examples of how cultural forces might influence the operation of these ecosystems. The answer key is in the back.[95]

While all four patterns are interesting and useful for getting work done, the network model has a unique combination of characteristics: notions of flow, connection, and resilience are key collaboration elements, and they thrive in the network model. It's no coincidence that this is the operative cultural model for the Internet and all social media, which is why I believe public collaboration tends to break out so easily there. The Internet lacks cultural barriers that serve to constrain collaboration within organizations struggling to collaborate as effectively inside the firewall.[96] The other three cultural types—command, function, and practitioner—have elements that are generally in conflict with a collaborative mode of interaction. Here's a brief synopsis of challenges within each model:

- **Command.** This model relies on top-down instructions to ensure results will be carried out. While this mode of operation is often critical in a pure form, overuse in non-crisis settings can result in failed collaboration. This model is dominant in commercial board room environments and is also common in entrepreneurial start-ups and small businesses. In practice, strong hierarchical influences must be suspended or somehow moderated for true collaboration to take place. A key enabler is true empowerment.

- **Function/Control.** Increasingly prevalent across Western society and throughout corporate America, this is the only model that works well with scale.[97] As organizations grow, distributing tasks among functionally aligned groups of experts is typically the most efficient way to get work done. However, this is the foundation for the silo structure, which makes collaboration very difficult. It's often recognized and described as bureaucracy. This model is quite prevalent in both commercial and public domains. Hoarding and control of information drive the flow of power. It also brings a deep preoccupation with protecting the status quo, a form of survival. The pervasive existence of this model is one of the main barriers to effective collaboration.[98]

- **Network.** This model tends to thrive on the exchange of inputs, and works well for collaboration. Many traditional R&D departments and Customer Service functions are modeled on this type of cross-functional team. If the group's membership is diverse and connections become resilient (or long-lasting), this can be an effective means of information exchange that leads to new outcomes. Collaborative teams should seek to leverage this model. In virtual collaboration, this is the predominant platform for interaction.

- **Practitioner.** This model favors local creativity and an entrepreneurial approach to problem solving. While introducing flexibility, there's typically insufficient structure, process, or critical mass to enable true collaboration. This model is common in non-profits, offices of independent professionals (e.g., lawyers, dentists) and loosely organized small businesses.

Let's explore the functional/control model in more detail. It's the one associated with organizational silos, and routinely cited (by me, and others) as a barrier to collaboration.[99] Removing silos outright is often described as a cure, but I believe this is generally unrealistic. Most silos have become structural elements, designed into the organization and deeply embedded in its operation. The true challenge becomes one of information exchange across silo boundaries. With the classic R&D approach, collaboration can get isolated in its own silo.[100] I contend this is not scalable. Allowing any one silo to house collaboration is a death sentence to true organization-wide learning.

As discussed in Chapter 8, fears prevent collaborative flow in negative cultures when mistakes are not condoned, or where punishments are visibly meted out. Chris Argyris is one of the earliest organizational theorists to grapple with the topic of "unspeakable" matters in the modern organization, in an effort to loosen the stranglehold that negative cultures can have in some companies.[101] Some years later, Ikujiro Nonaka brought these topics to the surface once again, in the context of Knowledge Management (KM). Nonaka pointed out the latent desire of individuals to collaborate and share their knowledge, but articulated the role that power and fear continued to play.[102]

A discussion of cultural dynamics is valuable to any organization seeking to collaborate, since virtually all participants will be influenced by these dynamics. Various combinations can be discussed, and approaches for collaborating within each type of culture (or subculture) can be explored in-depth. Generally, due to the way it evolves, culture can't be changed by an arbitrary decision of leaders (i.e., a top-down approach). For adoption, an organization's members have to see evidence of a change and believe in its long-term prospects, regardless of who mandates it.[103]

As a local, near-term alternative, influencing culture in smaller collaborative organizational teams or groups is often the more realistic approach.[104] Specific groups that are empowered for risk-taking may flourish if an innovation sub-culture can be established. This approach is not unlike what has been achieved through corporate R&D or entrepreneurial spin-offs and divestitures.

This is precisely the strategy employed by Qualex, a division of Eastman Kodak, when new On-Site photo minilabs began to compete for rolls of film with the more mature Qualex overnight photo-finishing business in the early 1990's. To ensure the fledgling On-Site Processing (OSP) business would have freedom to innovate and expand as needed, the division was spun-out of the core Qualex operating unit. Ultimately, Qualex created a versatile portfolio of options for Kodak's retailers. The culture of the spun-off division was fundamentally different from the overnight business, allowing OSP to adapt to the changing needs of a retail-facing model.

Any organization or group of people seeking effective collaboration must take steps to foster a culture of learning and sharing that must include strong elements of trust, respect for others, open communication, risk taking, and knowledge exchange. All four of Handy's cultural models are viable but collaboration fares differently in each. Understanding these factors and taking conscious action on any of them is no small task. It must start with leadership, be embraced by the entire organization, and be supported by constant reinforcement. Change must be anchored in the daily operations. Everyone must be able to see themselves in the future state, and they must be actively enrolled in pursuing that outcome. Command and control is a dated model, and it's slowly giving way to new thinking, as companies realize that a hierarchy driven model is counter-culture to collaboration.[105]

I'm convinced that negative, self-defeating cultural forces are a fundamental problem in the 21st Century organization. If the Industrial Revolution fostered cultures where specialists in silos are the norm, collaborative behaviors have become the exception. Achieving effective, ubiquitous collaboration in modern organizations will only occur when there's strong cultural reinforcement. There must be a culture of learning that advocates discovery, the sharing of knowledge, taking risks, and making mistakes.

In my consulting work, I've made significant inroads into the cultural challenges of my clients by sharing Handy's four models as shown in FIGURE 15, and discussing how they map onto the experience of specific organizations. So often, especially in the case of culture, it's simple awareness that sparks new ideas and new thinking.

TAKEAWAYS for "Culture"

Try to answer these questions in the context of your current organization, or organizations of which you've been an active part:

- **T1. Does your organization follow one specific cultural model? If so, can you observe characteristics consistent with Handy's model, or does your organization have more of a hybrid pattern?**
- **T2. Are there subcultures within your organization that exhibit some of these tendencies?**
- **T3. What specific cultural or organizational characteristics can you relate to as an individual? Which, if any, represent a personal conflict for you?**
- **T4. Which elements in Handy's model prove healthy and which ones do not?**

The next two chapters focus on relationships. Culture plays a key role in guiding our behaviors. In many cases, we'll find that cultural forces are working against us. We'll need to become very well informed about the dynamics of culture, if collaboration is to have a fighting chance.

11 – Contrarians

On Ego, Power and Control

Living alone—the life of a hermit—may still be possible on a deserted island, but I doubt you'll find it anywhere else. In the 21st Century, an insulated, "make your own rules" existence is rare indeed, especially within the modern organization. Even independent consultants and solo practitioners must adapt to the rules of their industry and their customers. Like an old school game of pinball, our hyper-connected world accelerates us in the direction of others, landing us shoulder-to-shoulder and sometimes face-to-face with all sorts of interesting, curious, and even unruly individuals.

I think it's fair to say that, given a preference, most of us want to get along. Psychologists are pretty clear on this point. They tell us that humans seek relationships that make us feel secure and connected, and will seek to avoid those that seem threatening.[106]

In organizations, the same goal applies, though our chances are constrained, with barriers amplified by scale: in the corporate world, we face high numbers, close proximity and extended durations. And it's hard for us to influence much of this. When we take a job or join a new team we're playing the relationship lottery, hoping we'll get to work with a boss who actually understands us, with coworkers and colleagues who value us as individuals. If we're apt to be more realistic, most will gladly settle for a pleasant work environment, a place with a functioning source of coffee where we look forward to coming to work each morning.

Sadly, even that sounds a bit utopian.

Why is finding a viable workplace so difficult?

The motivations for antisocial behavior are many. For individual cases, it can be driven by short-term frustrations that are often cyclical, focused on workload, hours, or compensation. The need for better communication is often listed. Others seek more of a challenge.

But when we encounter collective or long-standing levels of unrest, something else is usually going on. It takes on different proportions and different flavors as you move from office to office, and company to company. But where there is perpetual churn and malaise we are likely to find pockets of individuals who harbor unhealthy levels of personal ego, power, and what ultimately shows up as a desire to control. If these dysfunctional forces gain critical mass, they can be deadly to the functioning of a collaborating team, not to mention the organization at large.

As we've discussed, most of us have a strong fear of failure and its reciprocal, a strong drive to survive. These have become part of our organizational culture in many cases, with the rules of engagement stamped on our psyche: we can rock the boat if we want, but in the end, we're likely to pay the price with a pink slip. The ongoing struggle for organizational survival is rampant in large bureaucratic environments, where the very mission of the culture to protect the status quo, in spite of troubled economics. As told by Chris Argyris, fear itself often lurks behind the scenes as an unspeakable issue, and a host of organizational thought leaders concur that these problems can reach serious levels if unchecked.[107]

The forces of ego, power and control aren't all bad on their own merits, of course. Each can prove harmless in a natural state. Ego in psychology is our personal sense of self, defining boundaries about who we are. The boundaries might be healthy or unhealthy, but ego boundaries alone will not sway malaise in an organization. Power is also normal in human affairs, defining how leaders influence a body of people; power accrues to leaders who—if they don't abuse it—wield their influence to lead and facilitate change.[108] Control is a vital element across many industries and job functions, including almost all aspects of engineering, accounting, and manufacturing. It's the science of seeking certainty, removing exceptions and variance, and formulating important processes that drive safety, efficiency, and economic value—factors that contribute directly to the bottom line.

So we shouldn't generalize about the scope of the problem, or the three causal factors that this chapter brings into focus. But the point remains. Collaborators routinely face significant hurdles in this space that we can't afford to ignore.

To isolate our challenges in the collaboration context, we must be specific, and look a bit deeper at what happens in collaboration practice.

Ego, power and control represent three elements of *dysfunctional behavior* in organizations, and they have clear symptoms. Communication falters. Relationships become strained. Morale plummets. If we personally feel disrespected, diminished, or otherwise put down in the course of these interactions, we tend to react by shutting down or turning away. From the perspective of social or interpersonal reactions, there is likely to be a fight-or-flight response.[109]

Collaboration is impossible under these conditions.

Though we might want to intervene, in most cases we really can't do enough to influence the actions of others.

So, over time, individuals in an organization learn to maneuver within these group dynamics, with avoidance the most commonly chosen path. Not all will master the delicate balancing act that healthy social interaction requires. But most know the drill, and follow it with precision.

People driven by a bias for power or control can disrupt collaborative teams if allowed to do so. They tend to dominate communication. They routinely block the evolution of synergies and the free flow of information essential to the exchange of good ideas. Addressing challenges like these is exceedingly difficult and can become a significant roadblock.

Are we dead in the water here? Do we have options?

We're not helpless, as it turns out. First and foremost, we can get smarter as to how we respond. We can't change the actions of others, but we can clearly determine our response, and perhaps even the response of our colleagues. Our job is to keep the flow and positive energy alive. Ultimately, we can focus on one goal that we can share and embrace, and keep top of mind in our day to day affairs:

Good team dynamics depend on healthy boundaries.

Let's say one of our co-workers continues to act out when we try to collaborate. Or should we up the ante? Let's say it's our department head.

The collaborating team is fully within its bounds to define the behavioral norms required for that group to function. Think of it as an island of normalcy, carved out of the surrounding chaos. Any behaviors that conflict with the group's stated charter are out of bounds, and will cause the group to fail. It's really the only jurisdiction that a collaborating team can claim for itself. At the door (virtual or otherwise), a sign might read:

"Abandon control, all ye who enter here."

Collaboration works when we allow the flow of new and creative ideas, when we have the opportunity to interact with other thinkers, allowing ideas to co-mingle in new and interesting ways. Attempting to control that flow brings collaboration to a complete stop. The possibilities of what can be accomplished evaporate. To protect our chances, it is important that the entire team—not just one member, or two, or the leader, but everyone—embraces the flow of insight among the team. We must deny control to anyone who would stake claim it. And that applies to the topic, the agenda, the ground rules, the flow of conversation, and the development of group takeaways.

Can dysfunctional behaviors among members eventually change? Psychologists would say yes, but it depends on a number of variables, and due to the timeframes involved, I wouldn't count on changes in the near term. Becoming aware of such problems is always the first step, but working through the many steps that lie beneath controlling behaviors can take months or years.[110]

If the traits are more situational, however, perhaps driven by short-term factors or faulty assumptions, the drivers may be influenced in the near term by changes in understanding and changes in perception. This involves removing fears of reprisal or any other drivers that may appear punitive. A collaborative subculture may be setup that creates islands of open exchange, with just enough safe space locally to allow dialogue. As I've said, humans are social creatures. Our collective desire to connect and relate with others is incredibly powerful. Where there is passion, the forces of fear and resistance can be overcome. In the words of John Hagel, "Passion guides and focuses our choices – it defines our trajectory."[111]

Like so many elements of Collaboration DNA, key factors like our motivations and relationships—and the people skills that enable them—never quite get on our radar. Like DNA, it's in our nature and it influences everything we do, but we can't see it and we tend not to think about it. We talk about passion and positive energy, but we're at a loss to pinpoint its source within our organizations and to advance its cause. We sense that something is working or not working, but we typically don't have words to describe it.

Collaboration requires competence in all things relational.

I've mentioned Daniel Goleman in past chapters, but we're going to tap his work even more heavily in this chapter and the next one, because his perspectives on psychology are so well aligned with what we need to know. He is a widely-read psychologist who has advanced public awareness of how emotions and social skills are connected, much of it now linked to an evolving understanding of neuroscience. He has offered compelling insights on how our emotions factor into our thought processes, starting with *Emotional Intelligence* (1995), and later, building on these concepts in business, with *Primal Leadership* (2002). Both of these works provide an excellent foundation for modern psychology in practical terms. More recently, *Social Intelligence* (2006) has taken the discussion still further into our collaboration conversation, building on ideas about social awareness and fueled by ongoing fMRI research. These advancements are incredibly useful, since we're at last gaining some awareness of how and why humans behave the way they do.

Human behavior, of course, is complex. There are no simple solutions to navigate these challenges.

To make some headway, let's establish some basics.

We've mentioned healthy boundaries and leaving our problems at the door. These ideas are fundamental, and a great frame for attacking collaboration. To get to advanced collaboration levels means making tough choices and many personal commitments. Raise the bar on expectations. Clearly articulate what is expected. Most will opt-out if they don't think the dynamic will work for them. This is a process designed to enable self-organization, a stakeholders' ability to decide whether or not to participate. In fact, self-organization can be highly effective to align stakeholders and weed out dissenters, because the process itself seeks to establish common ground.

The best time to fine-tune participation is up front, before the collaboration actually starts. It's a matter of prequalification, coupling very clear expectations with a means to allow participants to "opt-in" or "opt out" of the process altogether. In this way, anyone who enters the collaboration will have a crystal clear understanding of what's expected. A commitment to work within and adapt to the demands of a high-energy team must be verbalized and accepted. Only then will the group leader have enough leverage downstream to tap a member on the shoulder and say, "*I thought we had a deal?*"

This is a challenging area, fraught with land mines and sensitive subjects. To get better at how we deal with them, let's touch on some negative social interaction patterns, taken from Goleman. These are some circumstances worth avoiding, described from a collaborative point of view. Whether collaboration can move forward under strained or dysfunctional conditions depends on the skills of the various contributors, and to some degree on the training of the leader. The factors in FIGURE 16 spell trouble.

	Goleman: Negative Interpersonal Dynamics Implications for Collaboration		
1	**Fear of Social Rejection** – One of the most common causes of anxiety; a significant factor in group dynamics and a major barrier in effective collaboration.
2	**Flooding** – Experiencing an intense 'fight or flight' reaction associated with a severe challenge, crisis or expression of contempt.
3	**Hijacking** – The effect of anxiety eroding mental abilities; our emotions take over and we lose our ability to think clearly.
4	**Projection** – The tendency to believe that other people act, feel or believe the way we do.

FIGURE 16—Negative Interpersonal Dynamics
Assessment of key drivers, from Goleman (2002/2006)[112]

Only the very strongest teams can survive the intense resistance that stems from these dynamics. This sobering fact alone should be sufficient to make this a key are for focus.

TAKEAWAYS for "Contrarians"

Find ways for everyone to be aware of social dynamics. Give each team member an offline, private opportunity to opt in or opt out of collaboration. Those who don't want to play in an open collaborative forum don't have to. Here are areas to help bring the above dynamics into focus:

- **T1. Take Social Rejection off the table. The best way to avoid this is to make it off-limits; communicate a no-fail, no-rejection policy. What else can be done to ensure new members don't fear this outcome?**

- **T2. Alert group to Flooding as "talking over." A common way for emotion can take over a healthy brainstorm is when one person refuses to let go of the floor. Review Chapter 8. What else can you do to limit member talk time, or to head off a speech that becomes an emotional tirade?**

- **T3. Emotional Hi-Jacking and Projection (both difficult to catch). These forces act in the subconscious, and happen without our awareness. How can you detect these situations within yourself? In others? What techniques might bring these top of mind?**

Don't forget, functional results cannot emerge from dysfunctional teams, but significant amounts of energy and valuable group time can be consumed in trying.

12 – The Trusting Organization

Trust is a critical aspect of establishing any close relationship. In turn, it's a fundamental requirement to achieve *any* level of meaningful collaboration. There's really no other way to say it. I think most people will agree on this one. The challenge lies in learning to make it happen.

What does it takes to trust and be trusted?

Don't forget, once there, the battle isn't over; there's lots of work to keep it.

And as we've discussed throughout *The DNA of Collaboration*, what can be challenging for a two-person relationship gets considerably more complex as team size grows.

The goal of a trusting organization is ambitious, indeed.

I've found that our personal success in building trusting relationships is grounded, if not somewhat bounded, by the degree to which we're on good terms with ourselves. With limited self-respect or self-confidence, it's difficult to have a full and healthy respect for others, or to have confidence in their abilities. This is because we tend to project our own interpretations and limitations onto the other person, as we covered in the last chapter. It may not be fair, or even logical, but these behaviors are part of our human nature. We see other people through the lenses that we've long used to examine ourselves. If there are flaws in our internal vision, something far less perfect than 20-20, so to speak, those flaws are quickly and easily extended to how we perceive others.

Trust is no different.

In fact, trust builds on so many component characteristics that building organizations that are truly trusting is a remarkable accomplishment. It's a goal that many leaders aspire to reach. Any way you choose to attack it, it's a significant amount of work.

Stephen M.R. Covey has done the deepest dive in this area, working to inventory the many factors needed to establish trust across organizations and among team members. His book *Speed of Trust* (2006) provides us with valuable insights, helping us to understand the forces that contribute to healthy, trusting relationships. Whether or not you agree with Covey across the board, his perspectives are well worth reflection. As we look at trust in the collaborative context, I find that his 4 Core "Pillars of Trust" provide us with strong foundational materials. We've already covered Intention in Chapter 4, because it's so fundamental to our collaborative design, but we'll look at it again here in the context of Covey's model: [113]

- **We trust and respect people with *integrity*.**
  Covey defines integrity as the aspect of
  individual character that reflects a combination
  of congruence, humility and courage, while
  having an ability to remain consistent and
  honest; he includes follow-through on
  commitments, being open minded, and having
  core values as an ethical "center." It's a broad
  and complex definition, with the bar set high. If
  we accept even a portion of his definition (and I
  accept all of it) it's clear why so many struggle to
  get there. Whatever our ultimate personal
  standard, we must realize that integrity is a
  foundation not only for trust, but a key factor in
  the level of respect we hold for and receive from
  other individuals. We can attempt to collaborate
  without respect, but we will be cautious and
  guarded in our interactions; our ability to trust
  our colleagues will be bounded, limiting our

willingness to take risks, and severely constraining what is possible.

- **We trust people if we understand and can validate their *intent*.** Covey breaks down intent in various ways, but he ultimately holds with a conventional definition of intent as a "plan" or "purpose." He notes that misperception of intent can be highly destructive to trust. For collaboration, as we discussed in Chapter 4, the concept of intention implies "acting with purpose" as opposed to acting without it, which is tantamount to simply reacting to events around us. Declaring our collaborative intention (both as individuals and as a team) is critical to avoiding the common risk of misperception. The danger of projecting our shortcomings onto others remains. In this light, it may be clear why open communication is so important to trust; it's a matter of continually signaling, reinforcing, and gaining consensus on intent. In a relationship or on a larger team, this information must flow smoothly in both directions.

- **We trust people who are *capable*.** While Covey has a diverse breakdown of contributing elements (summed up in his "TASKS" acronym), I think collaborators can simplify the talent equation down to skills and knowledge. With motivated learners as collaborators, of course, the sum of our capabilities is never a fixed quantity. Again, Carol Dweck's view of the growth mindset comes to the fore. We're always learning, and the collaboration process itself ends up being a tremendous learning environment. With the intention to learn, our capabilities can always improve, often dramatically, reinforced by the synergistic dynamic of teams that are working together and learning together.

- **We trust people who can produce *results*.** As the old saying goes "results speak for themselves" and Covey did not move the ball forward here, though I'm not sure he needed to. Results can be difficult for a collaboration team to measure early on. Progress on collaborative capability (per the Readiness Model, covered in Chapters 4 and 18) will demonstrate momentum and an increased capacity for problem-solving. Taking inventory of insights and ideas generated is a good interim report card. Ultimately the outcomes produced by the team will demonstrate what it's capable of producing.

According to Covey's formula, trust requires strong character and competence, which seems to resonate in a common-sense way: "*I know John can do this. He doesn't want to let me down. If he consistently demonstrates his integrity, intention, capabilities and results to me, I'll continue to trust him.*" Note the conditional, "if." Trust is something that we must not only earn once, but keep earning over time.

Why Organizations Struggle

We know from both Goleman and Covey that we, as individuals, struggle to meet our own high standards, especially in the context of today's relatively complex organizations. Demands are high. If we don't meet our own expectations or those of our management, it's difficult for us to value or relate to the pursuit of character and competence in others, let alone an entire team. We become and remain obsessed with our own stake.

The trust dynamic compounds quickly, especially in a negative, challenging, or high-stress environment. In these places, situations will easily spiral out of control, and trust all but disappears. Recall our discussion on fear for survival in

Chapter 9. If we find ourselves in a culture where individuals are consumed with trying to survive, we'll find tendencies for being defensive, withdrawn, possibly even controlling.

Who will we trust in this sort of environment? The grim reality is: very few people, if anyone. The circle draws closer, like a noose.

Where there is minimal or no trust, we cease to function as team players, even if doing so is not in our nature.

It doesn't help that negative forces in organizations tend to function beneath the surface. As Chris Argyris found in his extensive research in this area, notions of negativity and ill-feeling tend to be unspeakable and "off limits" in most organizations. That means trust, like the collaboration that depends on it, faces an uphill battle. Many in modern organizations are afraid of their prospects for long-term survival.

With corporate layoffs commonplace and visible increases in revolving-door employment, any thoughts of instability regarding work or career can be highly disconcerting. The silo model puts teams of specialists at odds with one another, since they must compete for limited resources, sometimes controlling whatever resources are gained, eventually seeking to optimize their part of the overall solution, even if it ends up sub-optimizing the whole.

Trust appears to be increasingly counter culture.

This cocktail of fear, defensiveness, and distrust is a daunting situation in the modern organization. Unpacking and addressing these complex dynamics is going to prove difficult. To me, the challenges are clear. The organization's leaders must engage, giving collaborators the charter and the support necessary for the organization to change course. As a collaborating team, we're at the epicenter of the new work approach. We have no choice but to take it on.

How We Can Change the Game

Digging out of this mess is going to start with awareness at top levels of the organization—and there must be engaged leaders in the discussion, coming to terms with the situation, advocating a collaborative approach, and empowering collaborative teams to transform the organization. Culture changes slowly, if ever, so there is no time to waste. We're better off starting immediately.

As catalysts and leaders, we can change the game locally and model alternative behaviors for the rest of the organization. It's classic Christensen, really: start locally and demonstrate what's possible.[114] With intention, acquired skills, and practice, we can take on the negative cultural forces via the newer, emergent subculture that we proactively help to create. We start with a local success at the team level, and work our way out (not up or down), *like a rhizome, expanding across the ground and establishing resilient root systems.* Unlocking and addressing the trust dynamic remains critical, of course. Fortunately, trust can move in both directions; if trust is lost, we can almost always, in time, get it back. Covey's bank account metaphor is central to his book: [115]

M19. Trust is like a Bank Account.
He is not *invested* in this relationship.
He *earned* my confidence by delivering.
I gave him *credit* for the depth of his research.

Leaders in these situations must focus relentlessly on the positive. How can we build a trusting organization? What's the path to a better place?

Leaders and collaborators must make personal trust deposits. We must demonstrate integrity and exhibit strong, team-oriented intention, bringing every shred of talent we have to bear on generating the necessary results. The ability for humans to forge trusting social connections quickly and efficiently will help us here. Fortunately, there are many psychological tools at our disposal, some of which we wield instinctively and subconsciously.

Covey, of course, doesn't have the last word on trust in organizations, and certainly not the first. Research in the important area of *service quality* during the 1980's identified many of the same trust and respect drivers—among them *competence* and *reliability*—but at the time, they were surfaced in the value equation between customers and service providers; it is foundational research that continues to inform organizations today.[116]

What other dimensions of trust are worth focus?

Let's return to the psychological perspective. Again, we'll highlight a few of the tools in the collaborator's toolkit provided by Goleman. He calls out the interpersonal skills that work in a positive direction. In my experience, these can be used to full advantage in driving positive group dynamics:

	Goleman: Positive Interpersonal Dynamics Implications for Collaboration
1	**Limbic Lock** -- A direct, positive brain-to-brain connection between people demonstrating deep engagement, often signaled by eye contact and laughter. If we engage directly with others, we can work together at fundamentally deeper levels.
2	**Meme Emergence** -- Modeled on a gene, represents an idea that replicates as it gets passed from person to person, often through low-road emotional influences. Momentum is often built within a group in this subtle but powerful way.
3	**Open Loop** or **Mirroring** -- Emotional influence, "shifting into the register" of those around us. Bringing a positive vibe is contagious.
4	**Rapport** -- Mutual attention, a shared positive feeling, fueled by non-verbal signals. A sense that there is common ground being established that is worth advancing.
5	**Resonance** -- Skill of leaders to align and harmonize a group, also evident in collaborative teams who are 'in the zone.' This dynamic has more implications in the building of consensus around specific content or ideas

FIGURE 17 – Positive Interpersonal Dynamics
Assessment of impacts, from Goleman (2002/2006) [117]

Study the list in FIGURE 17 carefully. These are important ways to engage and forge stronger connections with others. All of these will prove valuable when we get to specific roles, team dynamics, and the collaboration process—key chapters ahead.

One final thought for practical application is to reflect on our approach for trusting people in new relationships. Where collaborative interaction is a goal, I've had success in creating a "bias for trust," essentially giving new contacts the *benefit of the doubt*. There is some risk here. But this approach is especially important given the power and scale of cultural forces that work against us in the modern organization.

We need to consistently model our desired behaviors and relationships. It's a long-term undertaking, which means there's truly no time like the present. Why wait?

TAKEAWAYS for "Trust"

Trust on a collaborating team is so fundamental that I often recommend starting on that dynamic first. What are the ways you help foster trust as a team member?

- **T1. Bias for Trust. This one is perhaps the most easily achieved, because it's in our personal power. Have you given someone the benefit of the doubt as a way to start a relationship? If they let you down, do you think can you'll be able to try again with the next person?**

- **T2. Positive Vibe: Eye Contact and Laughter. This is another way to create an upbeat place where trust can grow. Can you point to examples where you have done this? Is this a practice you can embrace going forward?**

- **T3. Communicating Intent.** Our ability to achieve (and retain) this comes down to being open and clear. What ways would you prefer that intent of a group to be communicated? How might this be kept up to date?

- **T4. Capability and Results.** Without the awkwardness of interviewing others, how might you determine their track record so that you might increase your confidence in them?

- **T5. Respect.** This is learned by most people before elementary school, but it's surprising how many adults don't have this sorted out. It is often best learned as healthy boundaries. How might you navigate respect issues that appear in a group?

Establishing trust is a responsibility of all on the team, not just the leader. It's so easy to lose and so hard to recover. When building a collaborating team, the many dimensions of trust need to stay top of mind.

PART 4: FLOW

*"A river is designed to
channel the flow of water ...
a leaf, the flow of nutrients."*

Beth Noveck

*"If you have people who
want to do something new,
create a place, an incubator
... a climate in which they
can innovate."*

Gary Hamel

13 – Space as Opportunity

The exchange of ideas requires a time and a place. When we come together to collaborate, even if we're stranded in the cramped corner of a cube or office, we're occupying a creative space. Can we concentrate? Can we focus? Can we capture what we come up with in a useful way? For better or worse, the space where we interact will have a direct bearing on the quality and depth of any collaboration that may (or may *not*) ensue.[118]

Collaboration depends on care in setting initial conditions.

For starters, we must choose our space wisely.

These days it's in vogue to advocate the pursuit of collaboration anytime and anywhere. There are many among the social media crowd who will seek to harvest the rich rewards of serendipitous encounters at all costs. It's almost as if planning and coordination has become the enemy of new thinking. After all, random meetings can yield bountiful fruit, however unpredictable it might be.

I won't rain on that parade.

I happen to like unpredictable fruit.

But I believe the level of thought that goes into our collaboration planning makes a difference. Our choices will impact our results. John Hagel calls intentional acts designed to create chance encounters a *serendipity funnel* and talks further about *exposing significant surface area*—tantamount to making ourselves available to others—as a means of fostering new connections and opportunities to collaborate.[119] In both metaphors—tapping notions of a *funnel* and a *surface*—I see powerful new ways to look at space requirements.

Intentional collaboration is a creative pursuit[120] and the time and space we allocate to creation nurturing of our newly formed ideas matters deeply.

Adding the requirement for flow raises the stakes.

Beth Noveck used the concept of *channels* to illustrate how nature finds ways to allow the transfer of natural resources; in her recent TED talk, she describes the flow of water in a river.[121] It's worth some reflection. Think about how rivers change over time: cutting deeper into rock via erosion, shifting due to sedimentation or flooding, following new channels cut by natural forces and human intervention alike. These are different but I think congruent aspects of our own River metaphor (M2). Noveck's usage calls to mind motion, choices, the need to overcome obstacles, and the opportunity for alternative outcomes. The river again proves to be a powerful way to think about both flow, as well as the dynamics of intentional collaboration.

Is there a venue that can handle such robust demands?

Let's look at our options.

If only by force of habit, collaboration in commercial environments usually happens in a conference room. We've all been in one of these. Typically we'll see a group of eight to twelve people, a leader, some flip charts, and ideally, a whiteboard with markers. While it's easy to turn our back on such archaic conventions, those flip charts and whiteboards are there for a reason. Creative emergence needs a place to unfold, just like an artist needs a canvas.

As we'll see in a moment, that space can now be physical or virtual, but in both cases, the same principle applies: *Any place we choose for communication can be a canvas for the exchange of ideas.*

The book, laptop, iPad, or Kindle in front of you right now is providing precisely that: a forum for the exchange of ideas. At the moment, reading these words is providing a one-way flow of insight. Since the invention of the printing press, reading is a time-tested way for authors to plant some creative seeds, and it's a fairly efficient means to get some new conversations started. Now fast forward 600 years and pay close attention. If you look, you'll find a subtle but powerful difference in how people can interact. Social platforms now allow the mass exchange of insights to become *two-way*, a capability that *fundamentally* changes the game as a vehicle for communication. This can't be overstated from my perspective. The implications are huge. Two-way conversations on this very subject matter have commenced on the book's website and on Twitter, as living evidence of this new trend.[122]

That's why this is not just a book, it's a conversation.

In terms of possibilities, this is a key inflection point.

But there's more.

I've found *time* itself is another fascinating and significant factor in our planning for collaboration. Our collective inability to manage or prioritize its use proves to be a continual challenge for most all of us. And as we've discussed, time is an increasingly scarce resource. We never seem to have enough, and it's proven difficult to bottle or manufacture.

There are essentially two aspects of time that enter into our collaborative planning:

Synchronous   *in the moment, or real-time;*
Asynchronous   *not in the moment, or happening at a later time*

As social creatures, most will turn first to communication that is in the moment, or synchronous. Deep in our DNA we prefer the feedback and the connection that a voice, a face or a live handshake affords. But in our breakneck 21st century, time pressures have shifted that preference toward the asynchronous mode, which for most people today is that bottomless holding tank of parked communication we call email. Most of us love to hate it. It's highly convenient, but a dreadfully difficult beast to tame. And of course, ultimately, it's a double edged sword. With email we lose the immediacy and positive feedback we need to communicate, but we buy ourselves some precious time to prioritize. Then we let that communication pile-up, and create a fundamentally different issue of backlog management. To solve one problem, we've created others.

I believe the flood of communication in the modern world has overwhelmed our sensibilities, and email has become a faulty safety valve. In the process, we've become desensitized to our need to engage in human interaction. After months or years of being buried in a bottomless "in-box," we find the direct interaction with others can seem strange indeed.

All of this spells trouble for collaborators, because both email and atrophied people skills have moved us apart, when we need to be moving closer together. And for all the telecommunication advances that produce more capacity delivered in less time, we have only increased the demand and dependency for email.

In FIGURE 18, I've taken some space to reflect on places where collaboration might happen—both physical (face-to-face) and virtual (electronic)—summarizing advantages and disadvantages. As you review this analysis, challenge your thinking about where collaboration is possible, take a few moments to reflect on the factors listed.

You may be surprised by all the nuances.

Many who collaborate on public platforms like Twitter or Google+ will find any notion of structure—including and in some cases especially, the mechanical details of process and place—to be utterly distasteful. The Internet and its various emerging social technologies thrive on a culture of openness.

It's almost a Wild West environment of "anything goes" and "rules are made to be broken."

Technology of course provides a continuum of options. At the low end of this evolution are traditional, ubiquitous communication devices with enhancements: conference phones with remote microphones, computers that take phone calls, elaborate video screens, all serving to expand the reach of the real-time brainstorm.

Comparing Collaboration Venues	Venue	Optimal	Pros	Cons
Face to Face Venue (F2F) In-Person Collaboration constrained by time and space (can participants be in the same place?)	Conference Room	●●	Space optimal Capture optimal Quiet for privacy / focus	
	Office	●	Quiet for privacy / focus Capture possible	Space may be limited
	Park w/ Picnic Table		Space plentiful Relaxing, low-key	Distractions (can be noisy) Capture difficult
	Golf Course, Sporting Event, Water Cooler or Break Room		Opportunistic Relaxing, low-key	Space inconsistent Distractions (can be noisy) Capture difficult / impossible
	Coffee Shop, Book Store	●	Opportunistic Relaxing, low-key Capture possible Internet access	Distractions (noisy)
Virtual Venue Electronic Collaboration including Social Technologies constrained by time	E-Mail		Ubiquitous	Difficult to manage flow Difficult to interpret intent Getting back to key insights Version control issues
	Conference Room w/ Bridge	●	Space optimal Capture Possible Quiet for privacy / focus	Difficult to hear & see everyone
	Blog Post, Wiki	●●	Space adequate Capture possible Opportunistic	Requires new mindset
	Twitter Chat, Skype or G+ Hangout	●	Opportunistic Focused Real-time	Space limited Capture difficult
	Twitter	●	Opportunistic Real-time	Difficult to sustain focus Space limited
	Facebook, LinkedIn, G+		Space adequate	Not focused Capture difficult

FIGURE 18 – F2F & Virtual Venues for Collaboration
Advantages and disadvantages to consider
good = ● optimal = ●●

At the high-end of this evolution are advanced collaboration platforms that leverage social platforms over the internet and their two-way sophistication, including Twitter, Google+ and Skype to name just a few examples. These solutions change the rules of reach, suspending the notion that you have to know your collaborators in advance.

Blog platforms offer a nice compromise among the portfolio of options, providing more structure, expansive space to provide more feedback, and a way to interact with readers via comments. This reflects well how we tend to interact in real life, providing significant *user experience* benefits; the more intuitive the technology, the more rapidly it will gain adoption. Their recognizable magazine look and subscription capability offer an intuitive place for a reader's eyes to land. I believe that blog platforms may provide the most scalable home for the expansion of social-based collaboration. It hasn't taken off in the enterprise as yet, but that may be just around the corner.

In both low-tech and high-tech scenarios, the most basic paradigms for communicating retain common elements: individuals come together and exchange information. But more and more, the venue for collaboration is transforming, evolving, and changing what is possible. The notion of flow becomes more intuitive in the shaping of our interactions. This introduces a paradigm shift that I believe is happening all around us, in the context of both communication and collaboration.[123]

For some, a leap of faith is required to understand or even acknowledge the existence of virtual collaboration. Two-way communication over long distances does not feel possible or comfortable for many. Our innate desire to connect in social settings drives a presumption of being face-to-face, which for some can be a deeply held requirement.

I clearly recall networking with a man who was adamant that it was impossible to make meaningful, engaged connections with other people who were not present in front of you. A handshake, he insisted, could not be replaced with anything electronic. The fact remains that I've done it. I've collaborated with, learned from, and become friends with talented individuals all around the world who I've never met in person. Connecting and collaborating can happen in virtual ways and folks are catching on. Time and technology can change things, if we open our minds to the possibilities.

Virtual collaboration is viable.

The question of scale may come to mind. Are there thresholds for an optimal number of participants? Design experts like Tim Brown of IDEO advocate smaller numbers to ensure engagement and to avoid communication overhead,[124] and I think there's a strong argument for this. Others in the innovation space agree.[125] But how small is small enough? A great many variables influence what the high-end participant limits might be, as shown in FIGURE 19.

Group Size Factors	Face to Face Exchange (In-Person Collaboration)		Virtual Exchange (Electronic Collaboration)	
Categories	Optimal Size	Rationale	Optimal Size	Rationale
Experienced team	8-12	Provide all participants with time to contribute; sound & line of sight can be constraints	15-20	Multi-threaded exchange. Format allows concurrent contribution; "talk over" not an issue for most
Passionate participants	6-8	Longer average talk time	12-15	
Less experienced team	5-8	Group more tentative, requires more time to learn, experiment	10-15	Group more tentative, requires more time
Walk-up, spontaneous, (including simple conversation)	2-5	Informal, any space available; group forms in the moment, around ideas of interest.	2-8	Group forms in the moment, around ideas of interest; can also be offline/async
Opportunistic public encounters (strangers welcome)	2-3	Serendipity runs high, but lack of preparation or tools tends to make productive outcomes unlikely	2-10	Unique to the virtual format afforded by social platforms, collaboration is open ended

FIGURE 19 – Target Collaborative Group Sizes
Assessment of optimal group sizes

Drivers include affinity among members, difficulty of the objective, and experience of the team. The physical vs. virtual dynamic enters in too, especially on the high-end.

There is no doubt in my mind that smaller teams drive a significantly higher level of intimacy. Communication is clearer, feedback loops are tighter, and the ability to drive consensus, simply based on the numbers, is higher. There are tradeoffs to be sure but in general:

Teams should be as small as possible, but not too small.

I believe a good working high-end number for face-to-face collaboration is 15. As a working average, I'm most comfortable in the 8-12 range. In a virtual space, like Twitter, it may be double that, due to simultaneous threading of conversations.

Twitter chats are an evolving collaboration medium conducted in the public domain, where thoughtful and engaged people can assemble to share their ideas on a particular topic. Participants use a *hashtag* (a keyword, prefixed with "#") to index and aggregate comments. In a sense, a virtual chat room is created, reminiscent of AOL and IRC decades before. As word of the Twitter chat gets out, people assemble to participate, or they drop by if they see tweets that they find interesting. A conversation emerges. Whole communities form. Recurring topics are scheduled weekly or monthly. When positive energy and useful insights are shared, a strong sense of value accrues for the participants.[126]

It shouldn't be a surprise that many keep coming back.

For those paying attention to these streams or even stumbling upon them, the value arises from not only new ideas or a place to expand upon old ones, but as an opportunity to interact with other insightful people. With some attention to structure and promoting the conversation, Twitter guarantees a steady flow of new stakeholders, attracted by an open, lively exchange of ideas. For all the value and power of the typical, physical, face-to-face exchange, the concept of networked learning and collaboration has begun to demonstrate its considerable potential.[127]

The Japanese have a word for collaboration space called *ba,* which Ikujiro Nonaka introduced to the West several years ago as a key concept in the sharing of knowledge. I will expand on it further in Chapter 19 as we discuss the evolution of Knowledge Management in the enterprise, but I'd be remiss not to mention it here. It's a powerful way to capture the concept of opportunity. I believe *ba* is an essential element of Collaboration DNA because it serves to unify and foster so many disparate elements in our discussion.

Most modern organizations lack creative opportunities to innovate. They are missing anything that resembles *ba.* The notable exception perhaps is Google, which advocates 20% white space on the clock for its employees to innovate and experiment.[128] For the rest of us, time is always too precious, competition for our time and attention too fierce, our deadlines too tight to allow for that much white space. And yet Google continues to expand and grow and dominate in its market. Is it time that holds us back? We have conference rooms, and we have the internet connecting us all together.

Are we prioritizing our time correctly?

Ultimately, we need the holistic picture: a collaboration space that provides a productive place and quality time. Optimal collaboration requires that we invest energy and attention to both. But back on the planning topic: what happened to *spontaneous*? Have we surrendered that?

By all means, don't lose an opportunity to interact in the moment. Collaborate where and when you can. Just be prepared to field the insights. We need to guard against letting spontaneity trump longer-term value, measured by how much insight we can retain. The ultimate compromise might be one of mobile note capture, the equivalent of an artist carrying a sketch pad tucked under the arm. I'm never far from my 4x4 sticky pads; random insights must work pretty hard to escape my capture. Intentional collaborators, like artists and photographers, may soon find themselves on creative alert, perpetually on call, more aware than ever of the constant deluge of opportunities (in terms of insight and ideas) flowing past them.

I think we can safely conclude there is no one best venue for collaborating. Choose the ones most suited to your style of work and your purpose at hand. Sometimes options will be limited. I always have a favorite destination in mind and a few back-ups on tap. What is my all-time favorite? No doubt it's my neighborhood coffee shop, where the bulk of this book was written, a space that was friendly and inviting, where more than a few spontaneous conversations emerged.

TAKEAWAYS for "Space"

In FIGURE 18, I listed many venues for collaboration. Evaluate whether you can expand and perhaps diversify the collaboration you are undertaking by trying places you had not considered before. Experiment!

- **T1. If you are a die-hard conference room collaborator—try one of many virtual options available to collaborate, and note any unexpected results**

- **T2. If you are consumed by social media collaboration—try using your current methods in a face-to-face forum that changes the rules, such as a conference room, park, or a coffee shop**

- **T3. Advocate virtual collaboration at your company—try using social networking features of available tools; common examples include Yammer, Tibbr, Clearspace, NewsGator, or Chatter. If your company doesn't have these tools, seek to**

> prototype their use on a low-cost "cloud"
> version for a strategic work group
- **T4. Try virtual collaboration via Twitter chat**—It could fundamentally change your view on the levels of collaboration that are possible

By trying different formats, the factors that drive results start to become clear. Capture looms ever more important on the list of needs. Virtual connections can limit important non-verbal feedback, but more and more, collaboration technologies help give us a leg up in other valuable ways.

14 – Key Roles in Collaboration

A curious thing happens when people come together in a group setting. It scarcely matters whether they're friends or family, acquaintances or strangers. It happens in business and social gatherings of all kinds. As long as there is some communication, a kind of negotiation takes place. The individuals find their comfortable place within the group. They start to play key roles.

How can this be? What's happening here?

Most experts believe the strong, inherent desire to be socially connected is the driving force, with an equally strong desire to be accepted; Goleman, Senge, and Wheatley have been vocal on these tendencies.[129]

For those seeking intentional collaboration, and especially for those leading it, there's significant value in understanding these dynamics. The most productive collaboration will be the one that brings together a healthy, balanced mix of contributors.[130] A group of all leaders and no followers will be of little more value than a group with all followers and no leaders. Like star football or baseball players coming onto the field, collaborators have developed certain skills and talents that play to their strengths.[131]

Most who are successful in this space know that *collaboration is a team sport.[132]*

Below I've listed the most common roles that emerge in a productive collaboration session. These are archetypes, model roles, derived from my personal experience. Those in the group who can multi-task might wear many of these hats at once, which is important for smaller teams. See if you can see yourself or others you know in the following descriptions:

- **Aggregator.** Responsible for capturing notes and takeaways, based on objectives established by the group.

- **Analyst.** A deep, logical thinker, a person who can take apart ideas to consider pros and cons, and who can assess the relevance of the topic at hand; they also help ensure that the topic being discussed isn't rushed through or taken for granted.

- **Catalyst.** Generally starts a debate, a new discussion thread, or simply the next big idea; differentiated from designers by their motivation to get things going in a social sense; a leadership role.

- **Challenger.** Likes to look at alternative conclusions, especially those that arrive to the group prefabricated; helps ensure that resulting assumptions are valid; sometimes considered a naysayer or devil's advocate; plays a valuable role by ensuring critical thinking.

- **Connector.** Good at making inferences, with a strong ability to draw together relationships among ideas that seem unrelated; excellent at identifying interesting synergies, similarities, or patterns across diverse contexts.

- **Designer.** Best identified by raw creative potential to come up with new ideas; also known for pattern matching, visualization, and a love for creating; often considered a "visionary" for their ability to see a future state that does not yet exist.

- **Historian.** Good command of already established knowledge, delivering insights during the conversation (real-time) or willing and able to research/reconcile material (offline) as needed; can also wear the badge of academic, researcher, or librarian.

- **Moderator.** Responsible for facilitating the session, guiding the content and flow of interaction, but actively listening to ideas, context shifts, and proposed outcomes; must effectively prioritize subsequent steps; a leadership role.

- **Planner.** Understands objectives and the collaboration process well; takes steps to ensure the necessary initial conditions and participants are in place; focuses on member recruitment and screening (if applicable); a leadership role.

- **Practitioner.** A person practicing, conducting, or otherwise carrying out the activities of a professional within a specific field; a critical but often overlooked participant!

- **Referee.** Monitors process guidelines and compliance, and insists on a clear, established approach; keeps the group on-track by periodically reminding the team of necessary boundaries. Focused on efficiency and schedule, to ensure time commitments are honored.

- **SME ("Subject Matter Expert").** A recognized authority in a specific field, serving as a "go to" within the team for immediate feedback on knowledge, trends, or open topics for the field in question (note: for effective collaboration, SMEs should be as open-minded and interdisciplinary in their thinking as possible; experts who are "dug in" and non-negotiable often struggle).

Collaboration can happen with some of these 12 roles absent, but productive, efficient, and high-value collaboration won't achieve ambitious objectives without the full complement of skills represented. Like any team in professional or recreational sports, leaving out key positions—perhaps due to penalties or injuries—spells disaster for the team's ability to function effectively.[133] To explore the impact for smaller groups with roles missing or shared, FIGURE 20 shows how smaller groups tend to subdivide the work flow, or more to the point, leave much of it out.

Collaboration Roles by Group Size	Small Group (2-4)	Small-to-Midsize Group (5-8)	Moderate Group (8-12)	Large Group (12+)
Leaders	Moderator Planner Catalyst	Moderator Planner Catalyst Referee	Moderator Planner	Moderator
				Planner
Idea Generators	Designer Analyst Challenger Connector Practitioner	Designer Analyst Challenger Practitioner	Designer Analyst	Designer
			Practitioner	SME Practitioner
Process Owners			Referee Aggregator	Referee
				Aggregator
Idea Curators		Connector	Connector Catalyst	Connector
				Catalyst
				Analyst
Quality Control		Historian	Historian Challenger	Historian
				Challenger
note: these roles often missing in smaller groups	*Aggregator Historian Referee SME*	*Aggregator SME*	*SME*	

FIGURE 20 – Shifting Roles with Team Size
Striking a balance, showing optimal group size of 8-12

Exercise caution in role-sharing. While wearing many hats is noble, it causes key collaborative activities to be spread thin, to the detriment of group outcomes. Even the best and brightest collaborators face a limit on their ability to play multiple roles, as we'll see in a moment. It's worth noting here that extroverted participants will tend to dominate the flow of dialogue, while those with an introverted nature may have fewer chances to contribute. The moderator plays a clear role here, working to ensure everyone in the group has the opportunity to provide input.

For any who desire to remain less verbal, several of the 12 collaboration roles are clearly more conducive to offline research or written follow-up. Collaboration affords roles for everyone. It's up to the Planner and/or Moderator to make sure individual strengths are mapped to the required roles as carefully as possible. From this diagram, some interesting observations jump out:

- **Small groups often go without key roles; only in the larger groups are all roles accounted for**
- **The degree of multi-tasking in very small collaborative groups is high; this directly reduces the effectiveness of participants**
- **More process focus is required as groups grow**
- **Lack of an aggregator within small, less process-intensive groups causes many important collaborative insights to be lost**
- **The natural grouping of roles shifts as groups gain in size and diversity; the value-added roles of idea-curation and quality control emerge with more focus and specialization**

The diversification of participants based on background and nature of expertise helps increase the chances of broad collaborative success, but there are no guarantees. We can "cast a wide net" and hope for the best, but planning is usually the better course.

TAKEAWAYS for "Roles"

Ultimately, each group will develop its own personality, and will strengthen its productivity over time by experimenting with different members in different roles. I've found that members will develop completely new skills and interests as the collaboration evolves, testing and expanding horizons and skill-sets in turn. As in most relationships, the ability to adapt brings the best chance for success, as opposed to keeping with rigid rules. Here are some things to try:

- **T1. Have members rotate into different roles.**

- **T2. Challenge members to try roles they feel less suited for; sometimes people believe they aren't qualified or able to do something that they haven't tried.**[134]

- **T3. Structure helps, but broader communities sometimes lack the focus and rigor that a structured collaboration team brings onto the field.**[135] **How can you inspire team members to play specific roles?**

- **T4. Look for creative ways to fill the Aggregator role; few want to take this on, as it pulls them out of the fray as contributors; this may be an ideal role to rotate through the group.**

Flexibility is important in navigating how roles are filled, over time. Applying old-fashioned give-and-take can go a very long way toward team buy-in, experimentation, and ultimately, the emergence of an optimal team dynamic, which is the topic we'll explore next.

15 – Team Dynamics

A Leader's Guide

We've discussed many collaborative barriers on the journey so far, ranging from language, to culture, to personal behaviors, to the nuances of cognitive neuroscience. Maybe that's why leaders stay so busy. Whether you're setting a direction for an organization, or setting the pace for a collaborative team, the fundamental dynamics in a group have common elements. Collaboration introduces challenges and pitfalls in almost every dimension, so it's important for leaders to take inventory and to have mitigations at the ready. Without help and guidance, most teams will struggle. Leaders must be visible and they must operate out in front, working to *clear the path* of obstacles that are sure to block the way.[136]

By now, it should be clear: humans are fundamentally social creatures, with complex mechanisms for interacting with others. It's a subtle, "always on" mode of behavior that we tend to categorize as *interpersonal skills*. Many find the dynamics deeply intuitive. For others, basic coaching can help. Either way, it's a critical area for focus.

Interpersonal skills are core to successful collaboration.

At the core of these skills is empathy, which people start experiencing around the age of two. But from there, our paths diverge. According to Goleman, we tend to follow one of two roads: either we learn to interact with others through an emotionally healthy set of interpersonal skills, or we learn to mask our feelings and become what he calls *natural actors*.[137] What we experience as team dynamics in our organizations is a mash-up of individual contributions that are infused with these deeper tendencies.

Some bring the healthy foundation and some do not.

In Part 3, we covered many of the individual-level skill-sets and the relational challenges that flow from them. Now we'll set those forces in motion, looking through the lens of collaboration in progress. As we do, we'll look for ways to monitor, guide, and influence the collaborative outcomes we seek.

Leadership as Art

Like the author, the poet, or the songwriter, a collaborator must inspire each listener to pay attention. The collaboration leader must raise the bar further, modeling target behaviors for others. They must always be listening to what is going on and guiding the team through challenging spots. It's a leadership role that takes on the skills of a maestro conductor:

> **M20. Collaboration is a Symphony.**[138]
> He *orchestrated* the meeting flawlessly.
> She *conducted* the session with flair and enthusiasm.
> The meeting closed in a *crescendo*, with a *roar of applause.*

A leader appreciates the intricacies of the interplay among the team, and guides members through difficult passages and helping them work out complex efforts to harmonize. They seek out and find common ground. They find ways to weave together the ideas of diverse members. Let's stay with musicians for a bit, because a successful band is an excellent example of collaboration in action. To create a professional sound, every musician must participate in crafting the finished product. It's about finding notes that work with chord progressions, lyrics that work in harmonies and fresh new riffs that flow through all of it. The band must collaborate closely to make their music come alive. Sure, there's always room for a few solos. But the hard work of a well-orchestrated sound falls on everyone in the group. Let's look at a case study.

Pines of Porter
Insights about Making Music

Pines of Porter is a new band based in Nashville. They're still working out their sound, but to me it seems headed to a place where folk and blue grass brush into mainstream pop. While only together a few months, they've already written 6 songs, recorded two demo tracks, and played their debut gig in St. Louis. I had the opportunity to participate in a recording session with them[139] and was impressed by how well they worked together. Sensing they were onto some collaborative magic, I talked with the four of them— Taylor Berryhill, Derek Cohen, Corey Jones, and Courtney Kruckeberg—about what was behind their early success.

As they talked, respect and friendship were common themes, and a balance of hard work and fun. But in the studio, as I watched them work, I was struck by their level of focus. Many bands are immersed in the financial pressures of trying to make a living, or they become deeply consumed by the technical mechanics of their craft. But *Pines of Porter* seemed able to focus on demand, bringing professional energy to the tasks at hand, but they did so without losing their sense of humor. Somehow they are able to balance the hard work of professionals with the fun that they have making music together.

"Based on our training," said Derek, "we know we're

here to accomplish something, and we know that being focused is important." Corey agreed, adding: "When something's not right, we all know it."

Time and again, that dynamic seemed to bring their creative energies center stage.

Corey put it like this: "We have the same view of where we want our music to go. So when a new song starts coming to life, the whole band wants to invest in the creative process." Derek added "there's no reward like doing it on your own terms, with something that you helped create."

For Courtney, the best times have been when everything seemed to click: "There really are no words to describe that moment. A deep smile comes over me, and I just know our hard work is paying off."

Though the band members are all relatively new to Nashville, they're serious about their music. Some have been professionally trained and some are working in the industry, but all have deep experience as musicians. That's an important source of common ground. Derek pointed to several factors that put the group on equal footing but he said the most important has been the level of commitment. "There's a strong shared desire to see where this can go. How can this develop? What can we do? What can we give to the world that's unique?"

Among *Pines* members, the focus on *possibilities* is universal.

The personal connections among members are strong and visible as well. "There's friendship at the core of this," said Taylor, and they all agreed. To Derek and Corey, another key element has been strong mutual respect. Corey continued, "We learn from each other and support each other. If one of us is trying to learn something new, the band is supportive." I saw it first hand during the recording session. Despite their relatively deep experience base, no one ever played the expert card. It seemed they were all there to get better, anxious to improve their skills and their craft, and ultimately, in Courtney's words, "to better our music."

As they recorded, I was impressed how fluidly they changed roles, taking turns at vocals, playing lead, and directing the work flow. And when it was time to make a change, there was open discussion. "We all have input," said Corey, "Everyone can make suggestions." He and Derek said some bands are driven by a strong personality that can cast the rest of the band into supporting roles, sometimes suppressing the creative dynamic. "This is different," said Corey. "Our energy now is in the creative process, and everyone is participating."

Watching them in the studio, that energy was palpable. During the 12-hour session, I saw no evidence of unspoken issues or concerns being swept under the carpet.

Their professional training seemed to serve them well.

Artists usually take great pride in their individual creations, so I asked them how they handled challenges to a lyric or riff they had personally written. "We don't get attached to things that aren't mature," said Corey, "It's all a work in progress." Everyone had stories to tell how they navigated the personal aspects of this, but when it came to *Pines*, their stories always converged: there would be a group discussion that resulted in an agreement. "Building consensus can be inefficient," Derek concluded, "but it usually ends up being best."

Corey and Taylor have brought in most of the new songs to date, but their writing styles are very different. Corey attacks his music starting with licks and leaves melodies until later, reflecting his early training in jazz. Taylor, coming from mainstream side, starts with the melody, and works in the opposite direction. That brings significant variety to their collective creative process.

Pines of Porter is just getting started, but they seem to have more early momentum than most new bands. From their insights, it is clearly driven by their talent, personal energy and their love of music. But I also believe it is fueled by their friendship, mutual respect and their collaborative approach. "We bring out the best in each other," said Derek, "it's a synergy that I can't put into words." Taylor summed it up: "I take pride in the art that we're creating—music that draws heavily on our many influences—yet is something all its own."

To me, what's happening within Pines of Porter is exciting, and it's a living example of collaboration in action. And it's a band I plan to follow. I want to see where all that creative energy might take them.

Margaret Wheatley continues to bring strong convictions to these social and collaborative dynamics, especially as they tend to play out among individuals who are part of a larger group. She notes:

> *"Once individuals link together, they become something different. Our world does not encourage separateness ... we expected a certain level of behavior, and instead we discovered unknown abilities."* [140]

I believe Wheatley is unique in her ability to paint the human dynamic as it's designed to be, rather than how it ends up playing out day-to-day. Her words breathe more meaning into the idea of intentional collaboration, extending the metaphors of flow and connectedness in powerful ways. It's about challenging individuals to become part of something bigger, and inspiring them to grow through the collective capability of the whole.

We see that dynamic playing out in *Pines of Porter.*

Wheatley remains a powerful voice in understanding and embracing not only collaboration, but also teamwork more broadly, organizational learning, community development, and, ultimately, social change.

It's important to note, these are forces that can scale.

Chemistry plays an important role in any successful collaboration. One bad apple may not spoil the whole bunch, but a lack of alignment, gaps in shared values, or an accumulation of diverging objectives can certainly be a recipe for problems.

Effective leadership has many dimensions, which invariably require a balancing act. Let's look at what we'll be facing as we seek to strike a healthy balance during collaboration.

Affinity aka "Getting Along"

Again, establishing common ground is an important foundation for stable team dynamics. Our social selves seek connectedness with others. How will people relate? What draws them together? What causes people to want to work in groups versus going it alone? How can we drive affinity in our collaborative organizations and teams?

What is this idea of *affinity* all about?

I've found six primary focus areas that are essential ingredients to team building.

- **Empathy.** Our ability to sense and respond to signals from those around us is powerful, and it sets a threshold on our ability to identify and tap into the emerging group dynamic.[141] Over time, tension may shift to anticipation, ambivalence may flow into excitement. Empathy puts us in the shoes of others, helping us come to a common ground from both sides.

- **Care.** At the core of human relations is a deep respect for the value of worth and others, which, for most of us, sparks a deep human desire to assist and support each other. This is likely rooted in the ancestral affinity tracing back, once again, to tribal loyalty and survival. Without this in the mix, other team-building skills might be present but members may lack sufficient motivation to drive to the needed result. We'll come back to the concept of care in Chapter 19, but it's an essential element.

- **Humility.** Bringing some vulnerability to the table is important when collaborative team building is required. It's the ability to say "I don't

need to be right. Maybe I can learn something."
It's a powerful equalizer. It suspends self for a
time, in favor of the group. When experts arrive
on the scene with all the answers, both affinity
and the esprit de corps of the group fall off,
almost immediately. Strong-minded, obsessive
individuals can have a disruptive impact on team
building as well; humility helps to offset this.[142]

- **Suspending Judgment.** Our culture has us
  deeply trained in the dichotomies of
  right/wrong, for/against, and winning/losing—
  ways of thinking that tend to polarize our
  thinking and lace it with emotional overtones.[143.]
  When team members cling to moral positions,
  their strong energies can serve to divide the
  team that needs to be united. Common ground is
  a place where such divisions are suspended for a
  time, to allow positive relationships to form that
  can handle the pull of diversity. This is especially
  important in the critical, early stages of the
  collaborative effort, when the group is
  establishing a rapport.

- **Personal Connections.** Teams are often thrust
  together and given deadlines. Background
  sharing is often relegated to traditional rituals
  like "ice-breaking" but these often fail to
  facilitate much information being exchanged.
  The longer the collaborative work stream, the
  more important and valuable the exchange. Pre-
  publishing a simple paragraph on member
  backgrounds and interests can help establish
  important connections on the front-end, and in a
  very efficient fashion. Affinities that may have
  been missed (had they been left to chance
  discovery) become apparent out of the gate.

- **Reinforcement.** Gaining verbal confirmation
  from others is one way we know that we're
  moving ahead in a productive manner. Making a
  big deal about progress creates strong support

from within the team and the resulting positive energy can feed upon itself, anchoring early wins and giving the group confidence to keep pushing forward.[144]

Keeping these factors in mind is essential for driving toward alignment in a collaborative group. If we can work these factors into our vocabulary and ground our conversations in these affinity-building concepts, our teams will benefit almost immediately.

I've found it helps for the group to work out affinity challenges in the open. If there are strong minded individuals or experts who resist buying-in, the group can and should speak out: "We value your input, but we want to be sure other positions are considered." If you're the expert, you can play a huge role in bridging the gulf, proactively offering: "Sure, I have depth in this space, so I may tend to tune out ideas that aren't in my knowledge base; challenge me if you see me doing that." Of course, at this point, experts should prepare to be challenged!

In my experience, affinity is the result of all the forces outlined here. It represents *common ground* in simple terms, but true affinity is achieved when connections are made at deep, genuine levels, beyond simply having things in common. It's not only about shared views, but about shared convictions, and a deep sense of mutual respect. Teams that have mastered these hurdles are able to move rapidly into the zone of collaboration, driving accelerated generation of insights, stepping through multiple contexts, and drawing new inferences and takeaways with dazzling speed.

Diversification

For all the value in group affinity, there is perhaps equal or even greater value in group diversification. This seems like a paradox. But when we realize the creative potential of opposing forces, celebrating diverse perspectives makes sense.

Again, this brings us back to the need for balance. Knowing a group can move too far in one direction may give us pause. Some new collaborators are tentative at first, trying to second-guess the winning meme, to interpret the desired tendency so they can filter their remarks. While the logic could be defended, this can constrain the flow of insight. I encourage groups to share freely and openly (when it's their turn, of course) and lean on moderation to strike the needed balance.

In the long run, of course, striking a balance is absolutely critical. Too much affinity and the group will begin to churn out repetitive material. Too much diversity and we will never accomplish anything.

Let's explore what we mean by diversity in the collaborative sense. There are many dimensions across which diversity can and should operate, including influences that are cultural, cognitive, professional, ethnic, and demographic. Groups comprised of members with a broad diversity among these categories are virtually certain to provide more robust outcomes, simply because their insights will be drawn from a broader base of experience. The diverse assessment of ideas will be more rigorous, with a better variety of contexts considered. The range of solution sets will be broader, fueled by the cross-pollination of so many diverse ideas.[145]

Perhaps most of all, group diversity drives greater resilience, giving diverse groups an edge. Their rich cross-sections of influence drive depth in thinking that has value well beyond the mere piling up of more ideas. Any weaker contributions by specific group members can be quickly bridged by stronger members. Groups can more easily survive the periodic absence of key players. Such groups can adapt more readily, and are more apt to produce emergent outcomes.

Affinity is important. But diversity is critical.

As is the case in all aspects of collaboration, finding the balance point is where the ultimate magic lies. And by the way, it's a moving target, constantly calling for new, more adaptive ways to guide outcomes.

Adaptive Governance

In our Western society and the culture that pervades it, the concept of oversight and management are closely intertwined, if not synonymous. Management is about delivering results, and oversight is making sure the managers are doing just that. Today, project managers can get certifications and can benefit from absorbing significant quantities of the official banks of knowledge,[146] but ultimately, a good manager must understand and apply standards, identify exceptions, issues, and risks, and implement the necessary controls to bring in a project on time and on budget. That's management-speak for minimal variance. Without question, it's a significant and valuable skill. When a structured, defined set of activities must be accomplished, managers must be engaged.

I've spent my career in roles like these. The value and energy of good management is in my blood, perhaps even in my own personal DNA.

But so deep are the presumptions about the role of a manager and the scope of management that countless books on management go to great lengths to define boundaries on exactly what needs to be managed and how it should be done. The area is full of prescriptions for process. It's a tale of structure on top of more structure. For delivering with precision on a schedule it is the proven path. But for solving difficult problems with cross-functional domain experts, new dynamics are called or. We must challenge some of these presumptions.

Complex problems require that we find ways to function with reduced obsession for structure.

Boundaries in our current day and age are beginning to move on us, if they were every truly there.[147] I've found that with many years of training and experience well-trained and experienced managers tend to manage, even when other courses of action might be more effective.

By semantic design, the concept of *governance* implies a broader, consensus-driven approach to the task of oversight than simple management by a single *manager,* or even a team of managers. It is less about direction and control and more about guidance. Governance introduces the concept of a committee of sorts, some representative group that comes together to provide the diverse perspective necessary to respond to changes and challenges. In the context of collaboration, this is a step in the right direction. But given the strong bias for process and control associated with most management roles and the managers who hold them, governance often takes the form of management by committee. Put a group of managers in a room, and you basically end up with lots of management. And most of it will harbor the top-down, role-based hierarchical structure that comes with it.

I'm a manager. I know how we roll.

Once again, success requires that we change how we approach the task at hand. Old habits die hard if they ever do, but effective collaboration will do best when not constrained by the planning and control instincts of a project manager.

So how might we approach the governance of collaboration? First, we must recognize two types of collaborative governance, authoritative and embedded.

- **Authoritative Governance**—sits outside the team, providing guidelines, boundaries, and objectives on behalf of the organization. Creative types and complexity advocates may denounce this attempt to control, but I see it as the reality of organizations. As a group (company, consortium, government body, etc.) we seek to accomplish something, and our leaders must often help create that contextual framework. In an organizational setting, this is part of the program.

- **Embedded Governance**—occurs when leaders are actually collaborating, whether as moderators or as contributors. This is a fascinating model that can be useful for culture rationalization, organization change, and strategy work, but it's not a model I've seen deployed that often. Where it's an option, I think the concerns levied against Authoritative Governance can be minimized; leaders are accessible, and part of the creative cycle.

Next, we can embrace the broader, consensus-based notion inherent in the term. What follows will assume the embedded governance approach, since it's the more interesting and advanced model and has more implications. Why a small "governing body" instead of managers? Here are some of the factors that influence this:

- **Diversification of perspectives**—strengthens the group's broad-based leadership view, providing a source of resilience

- **Providing loose but effective oversight for medium-to-large size groups**—especially if the group is virtual—can be daunting, while having two or three leaders playing active governance roles in real time can help

- **During collaboration, leaders may find the need to participate**—temporarily suspending their coordination roles and having depth in a governance structure allows for this. If a leader must withdraw due to personal reasons, or a conflict of interest develops; a collaboration led

>by a governance structure can keep moving
>forward

In today's world, the perceived notion of control—fueled by the deep process rigor required by good management practices—works against the give-and-take dynamics required for collaboration. Engagement and adaptation require space and freedom to develop organically. The forces of affinity and diversification bring a natural tension to the collaborative effort best left to the group to work through. When led by managers trained on schedules and control, the collaboration may finish on time, and the process might be followed to the letter. However, there may not have been sufficient time—call it spontaneity or white space—for insights to emerge and for ideas to combine and recombine in interesting ways.

Coming at the topic of oversight from the other direction—from the participant's point of view—poses an interesting question: *How much guidance—in the context of governance and/or management—would the group say it needs?* Owing to the depth and rigor a good manager brings to most every task, it may be natural to answer "none."

Skilled collaborators are quick to discern the dangers of control in a collaborative setting.

That said, I think abandoning managers completely is going too far in the other direction. The vast majority of collaborators in the world are likely to come from the ranks of management, so a bias for control and structure will be prevalent. This needs to be tackled head-on. Embedded governance is almost certainly the better oversight model than a single leader or facilitator, but even governance brings a presumption of structure.

A still better approach for collaboration is to introduce flexibility into the oversight by design, opening the oversight up to a broader, more collective influence by the group. The qualifier I like to use is *adaptive*. With that refinement, we have just enough oversight in place to let the group innovate without risk of control. Adaptive governance provides sufficient structure to frame problem and solution topics, to set and hold context throughout the discussion, and to keep some focus on results. But that's it. This model is neither prescriptive nor controlling.

As I've said, control will block collaborative efforts every time. Traditional management and governance structures may do the same. This is not to say managers will fail at collaboration. They should be welcomed to the table wholeheartedly. But they should be encouraged to suspend their deeply entrenched bias for structure and control. Attempting to apply it in collaborative settings will routinely create friction for themselves and for the rest of the group.

A well-trained professional facilitator understands these dynamics, and will take care to avoid heavy-handedness. While facilitators are often outsiders and generally not well-versed in the subject matter, they often play a critical and highly skilled role. Adaptive governance allows leaders within the target stakeholder group—many of them specialists or SMEs (subject matter experts)—to use their domain knowledge to help guide the effort, as long as it's balanced and does not dominate the outcomes.

The balance of affinity and diverse input falls squarely upon the leaders to guide, and the adaptive governance approach is how I've seen it work best.

We've covered lots of important ground in this chapter, which is why I subtitled it "A Leader's Guide," but collaborative teams are often great examples of participatory leadership, where groups essentially guide themselves. Mature groups (as I'll define in Chapter 18) can absolutely achieve this, but groups that are new or in the process of learning the approach need the extra guidance visible leadership affords.

TAKEAWAYS for "Team Dynamics"

How can you accelerate adoption of the self-governing model? Here are some things to try:

- **T1. Rotate leadership roles to all group members**

- **T2. Encourage the embedded governance model – where external organization leaders participate actively in the collaboration**

- **T3. Examine the impact of self-governing teams relative to existing cultural mores and norms in the organization. If self-governing would be considered counter-culture, devise steps that would lead to the necessary changes**

- **T4. Track the steps taken by moderators and leaders to balance affinity vs. diversity. Share the approach with the team. Often, the steps are intuitive to leaders and they are taken rapidly, sometimes with minimal conscious awareness**

Groups that share in the leadership capacity are functioning at a strategic level, indeed.

16 – Process

If the art of shipbuilding were in the
wood, said Aristotle, then stacking up a
pile of timber would cause a great ship
to rise up. What is needed for ships, he
argued, was a purpose, a design.[148]

Intentional collaboration is no different than Aristotle's hypothetical pile of wood. Collaboration requires a design. We must define what we seek, formulate a process, and set it in motion. A process doesn't have to be complicated, and it should not be over-engineered. In fact, quite the opposite is true. For collaboration to work in our fast-paced world it needs to be as simple as possible, something that can spring up on short notice. It must be lightweight, mobile yet scalable, flexible yet robust, open to serendipitous influences yet quickly transferable to a more rigorous approach.

It must come in small, medium, and large.

Those who collaborate on the Internet or who are steeped in complexity thinking are likely to argue against the need for process. After all, process is structure by definition, and many, including myself, have argued that structure can work against us. The culture of web-based social media is highly averse to formality, resisting formulaic or prescribed instructions for how things must work. The organic underpinning of complexity is similar, far more likely to propose a mantra of "let nature figure it out."

I'm all for spontaneity and natural evolution.

I still advocate for unpredictable fruit.

But structure for creative spaces within organizations is neither a paradox nor a flaw.

The challenge is that we're introducing collaboration—an intensely creative pursuit—into organizations that are fundamentally captive to presumptions of structure. I believe forward looking organizations need to grapple with this, seeking ways to work smaller, be more nimble, remove hierarchical controls, and, ultimately, function with less structure.

That doesn't happen tomorrow.

Intentional collaboration, in contrast, *can* happen tomorrow, but only if we adapt our creative instincts to something that will work in a less-than-creative environment.

In the business world there are many, many jobs to be done: products to launch, customer problems to be solved, and operational improvements to be made. Sure, we can create white space, step back, and hope for the best. But the better approach is to create white space and jump-start the innovation process with a lightweight collaboration model that will get people talking in productive ways.

Regardless of format, venue, or scale, there are some basic, very common steps that I want to expose here. FIGURE 21 shows how I approach lightweight collaboration. To anyone who has ever been in a group problem-solving session, some of these steps will look familiar. But I'll argue that there are common flaws to how we approach each step. Groups are prone to skip steps, get bogged down, or otherwise run off the rails at every step along the way. The simple, iterative process I've outlined here is designed to keep that from happening.

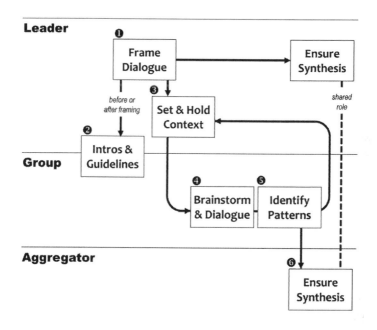

FIGURE 21 – Basic Collaboration Process, as a Flow
Core steps required to drive iterative collaboration
in either virtual or face-to-face formats; taken from
SMCHAT & ECOSYS (2009-2012) [149]

Let's review each major step in more detail, corresponding to the black circles, labeled 1-6.

[1] Framing

In this step, the overall objectives of the collaboration are communicated. Ideally, this is done in writing, in advance of the collaboration, so contributors can come prepared. Any new or difficult semantics are defined, problem dimensions are outlined, and objectives of the session at hand are stated clearly. Any background sources are cited and made available for reading

Real-time framing (during the session) can and should be done as succinctly and efficiently as possible to maximize the time available for problem solving.

For complex, multi-stage collaborations conducted over time[150] several special factors come into play, and are worth mentioning:

- **It helps to maintain a master plan so contributors can track those topics that are in scope and out of scope, per the session at hand**
- **There will be occasions to pull in topics from past or future sessions, but this should be done as an aside (like a footnote or "see also our discussion on"), without drawing the entire group into other topics. The moderator has responsibility for monitoring this common tendency to get sidetracked by bringing the primary discussion thread back into focus**
- **Periodic review of the overall framing is helpful to keep the end-goals in mind**
- **Quality time may be required for collaboration regarding the framing, itself; a group that contributes to the objectives will have considerably more ownership than when the topics are developed externally, by third parties**

For intentional collaboration, I do not believe there is significant value to entering into a collaborative session without framing. Quite simply, without a goal, significant results are unlikely. Participants will find it difficult to find and maintain a focus, since there is no means for aligning individual inputs with a purposeful, shared context. Accidents can happen, of course. But any useful insights that do emerge through random conversation are unlikely to survive the exchange. Although the conversation may be interesting and entertaining, with relationships formed and deepened, it won't be intentional collaboration.

[2] Introductions and Guidelines

While some may skip this step, it's important to establish a first-name basis for the team to interact, and also to get a sense of the relevant background of each contributor. This is less about ice-breakers (a time-tested way to get collaboration started) and more about informing the team about how individuals may be able to provide specific insight, expertise, or analysis, based on their background.

This step represents an investment by the group in its many person-to-person relationships. In combination, these relationships form the backbone of the collaborative dynamic, impacting the group's cohesion and overall affinity. The many positive elements of personal engagement (Chapter 12) and team dynamics (Chapter 15) can be set in motion and accelerated with focus and quality time on this step. Guidelines should be available for review on demand, but it helps to summarize them for new members, repeating them periodically during a long-running, serial collaboration. In the next chapter, FIGURE 25 provides a sample set.

[3] Setting and Holding Context

During a cross-functional collaboration, developing ideas will require the context of the conversation to change often. It's important for all collaborators to state context and to attempt to sustain it as alternative ideas are being offered and evaluated. In general, this is a key responsibility of the moderator, but everyone must understand the need and seek to track current context. Failure to do so can quickly result in loss of momentum and diminished value.

In practice, especially in public forums, keeping a group on topic is extremely difficult. Each contributor, often by design, will be bringing their own, unique portfolio of concerns, shaped by family heritage, culture, professional training, and/or personal bias, as we discussed in Chapter 10 (Dilemma of Culture) and Chapter 15 (Team Dynamics). The personal context of many members will be fundamentally different. This is the value of diversity and a key requirement for emergence, but it also complicates things for the group's moderators.

But we can't shy away from this requirement. Changing context during the collaboration is critical thinking in action. Ideally, contributors will be aware of the context change, and can state the change with their insight. But context changes can be subtle, and can creep into an insight, idea, or broader conversation unwittingly. For example, if a collaborative team was discussing the challenge of culture in public education, a context shift might be: "Let's spend a few minutes evaluating the cultural implications in a healthcare setting, to see what we might learn." By changing the perspective when evaluating a topic, new insights may emerge.

A strong collaboration team will become expert at navigating context changes, and won't rely on the moderator to do all of this important work. When I am playing the moderator role, I often enlist the help of several contributors to keep the context factor in mind. By sending pre-arranged cues to one to two lead speakers during the collaboration, some critical mass is there to help sway the rest of the crowd.

I've found that holding context during a lively chat is the most challenging role of a moderator. Both new moderators and new groups should avoid context changes in the middle of a conversation until they have built more accumulated experience. We'll look at the maturation process of a collaborative group just ahead, in Chapter 18.

It's important not to shy away from this over the long run, however. Like good framing, nimble context changes are fundamentally critical to the breadth, depth, and overall quality of the outcomes that can emerge.

[4] Brainstorm and Dialogue

This is the step where new insights are born, where ideas are fleshed out, and solutions begin to take shape. As in the popular movie *Inception*, this is the elusive point where magic happens. No surprise, then, that this is the most important step in the collaboration process and it should be allocated the greatest amount of time possible.

The most significant idea to take away about this step is the idea of *iteration*, the sense that the brainstorming of specific insights and ideas happens in waves, circling back to previous findings, to reevaluate what's been discussed with new learning and in alternate contexts. This is clearly represented in FIGURE 9.

Some who favor linear problem solving will be impatient with this. However, group learning and the creative process often function precisely in this manner.

Humans have a finite attention span, so the loop-backs can't go on forever. There are practical limits to the productive duration that a collaborative session or exchange can run. With the process outlined in this chapter, one hour is the minimum amount of time required to get momentum and accumulate new insights. A maximum is probably two-and-a-half hours, in part because of participants' need to take a bio break at about that interval.

In fact, at the level of biology and psychology, the impact that collaboration has on the body is less than trivial. Collaboration is hard work. The brain consumes calories just like muscles in the body, and like those muscles, after a stretch of exertion, it needs some rest. I've been part of many collaborative efforts where there was so much positive momentum that the group wanted to keep going. Those moments where the team is "in the zone" are rare, special, and definitely worth sustaining, but even in these cases, a periodic 10 to 15 minute break helps recharge the batteries.

[5] Identifying Patterns & Takeaways

How do we know when we're onto something important? Which insights and ideas have the greatest potential? These are open and debatable questions, a part of the creative process that makes collaboration so interesting.

One way to allow high potential insights and ideas to "bubble up" from the group is to observe how others respond to them. This is a particularly powerful aspect of virtual collaboration, because each input is self-documenting (often as a tweet) and ideas that resonate with other contributors are often clearly re-shared with others (via an "RT", or re-tweet). The moderator must keep a look out for insights or ideas that are getting significant traction, or conversely, sense when other insights or ideas are proving problematic or controversial.

Because new content can enter the flow at any point, the potential need to provide semantic clarity for those new elements is always lurking. A moderator must step in to help refine definitions whenever members of the group begin to struggle.

When will the discussion and brainstorming cycle have run its full course? That's a variable that must often float, and will ultimately fall to the moderator or referee to determine.

It's best to establish a time frame for the collaboration at the outset with minimum and maximum durations, so contributors can plan and confirm expectations and attendance, accordingly. The following factors signal the need for a wrap-up.

- **Max Time Exceeded**—It is important to make and keep commitments with the team; always try to end on time.
- **Fatigue Impacting Quality of Exchange**—If the quality and pace of dialogue is slowing down, the group is likely running out of steam; better to move toward a close and resume when everyone is fresh.
- **Loss of Critical Mass**—If too many participants depart early, the group will lack sufficient breadth and depth to function effectively; it may be best to reschedule a follow-up session, or move to a close.
- **Regrouping to Re-Frame**—Sometimes so much is learned during collaboration that the original frame has to be modified; unless change to scope and approach is slight, this will be very difficult to do accomplish in real-time; if framing or objectives need to change, it's time to regroup.

After working together for a while, a moderator and team will establish a natural rhythm that becomes intuitive to participants. Such familiarity drives more efficiency and lessens the monitor's orchestration burden.

[6] Synthesis

The most consistent point of failure in group collaboration is at the final stage, where takeaways are captured and inferences are made about priorities for follow-up. Most participants find it interesting to socialize, brainstorm, talk, and share ideas, but they seem to have little time for the fundamentally harder work required to make sense of it all, and to find ways to apply the most important elements for innovative solutions. I believe *synthesis* is the most important, fundamental step in the critical thinking process.[151]

Too often, key insights are lost, or they are merely catalogued through note taking and distributed in the form of a transcript. This means the only true value from collaboration will be individualized learning that results from group interaction, i.e., the simple transfer of insight from one person to another. This clearly has intrinsic value to participants. Personal learning feeds a hunger for more learning. This is reflected in the feedback loop in FIGURE 9. But this is not the end point, because it doesn't lead to the more robust, solution-focused outcomes that most collaborators seek. Where solution outcomes are desired, the synthesis step is critical, with the ability to produce longer-term value. A good example is the third Open Government Workshop, held in Washington during February 2010. The meeting notes achieved via inter-agency collaboration were posted to a wiki. As of this writing, they remain viewable online.[152]

A Structured View

With these planning and approach details sorted out, what's the overall set of activities required to orchestrate a formal collaboration? The following is a list of steps that could be used to structure a long-running series of collaborations, using the process detail described above, but adding additional steps for logistics and coordination.

For those seeking structure, I am happy to provide some here. An activity breakdown appears in FIGURE 22. As a manager with many years in the trenches, the story of collaboration in the organizational context would not be complete without a project plan. Again, my apologies go out to the web and complexity crowds, but collaboration in organizations needs to have enough structure to be recognizable. In matters of change, it's often best to adapt our solutions to the custom of local stakeholders, to achieve faster buy-in and participation.

When in Rome, do as the Romans do.

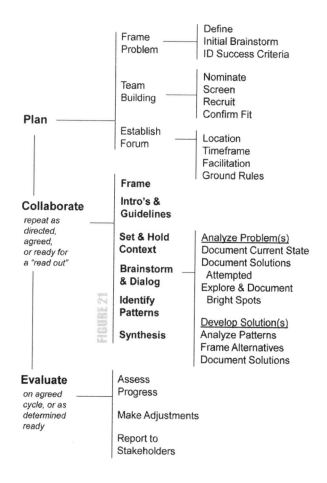

FIGURE 22 – Activity Breakdown for Intentional Collaboration
Holistic "all-in" view of steps required, including iteration

Setting it in Motion: Process in the context of Space

Experienced collaborators will already be asking: "How does our lightweight collaboration process apply—or more importantly, get changed—when the situational context of space changes?" Remember Chapter 13? We posed several modes of collaboration, including physical and virtual.

Does our process model work seamlessly in all of these? The short answer is yes. The long answer appears below, because physical and virtual settings change what's optimal. Let's look at some of the primary factors.

Scenario 1: Informal Approach.
Physical or Virtual; Minimal/No Process

When people gather informally and collaboration starts to happen, there are no moderators, process checklists, or other trappings to guide the discussion. People come together without a planned outcome, but they suddenly see value in coming up with one: "What could we accomplish if we brainstormed about X?" People (as would-be collaborators) essentially share what they have to share in whatever sequence appears logical. As I've said, most often the results from such an impromptu approach leave much, if not everything, to chance. What the group gains in raw simplicity is sacrificed on the back-end; useful outcomes are typically based on blind luck or the raw will power of participants.

But we can improve our chances.

I've distilled our quasi-formal collaboration process into several simple steps, worded in the context of an actual conversation. Following a script like this will lead to more thorough, high quality outcomes than the proverbial water cooler chat that's devoid of any planning, by definition. The speaker can be anyone in the assembled group, whether a formal or informal leader.

The speaking parts may also rotate around the group as well; it doesn't matter who makes the point, as long as the group is thinking along these lines:

Initial Spark or Trigger Comment (setting the stage):

"Hey, that's a great idea ... "
"You know, that makes me think ... "

Collaboration Beginning:

"What's possible from this conversation?"
"Can we establish some common ground on our direction?"

Collaboration Middle* (go around the group, repeating, as time allows):

"What are some insights you have on this topic?"
"What actionable ideas can we derive?"
"Do we see any patterns or similarities emerging?"
"What are some potential solutions to achieve our objective?"

Collaboration Wrap-up:

"There are some valuable takeaways here ... let's capture them"

That's it. A simple collaborative conversation, enhanced with some structure, but distilled down to the most basic components. Try to interject these statements during an informal but potentially valuable conversation on ideas, to see what happens. If two or three are interested and "play ball," you're likely to achieve far more value than you had ever imagined. If there's enough traction and energy that something could evolve, consider stepping up to the next level.

Scenario 2: Quasi-Formal Approach.
Physical or Virtual—Adaptive Model

A quasi-formal, adaptive approach is a bit more structured than the previous scenario, but it retains its open feel. It allows the group to make real-time adjustments that are essential for collaboration. I distilled this process model by helping it evolve in two different online communities, one focused on social media, and one focused on public education. The process worked well in a simple exchange of ideas, but it was increasingly critical when more difficult problems were taken on; these insights were among the core insights that led to this book.[153]

Why does virtual collaboration change the game?

The online collaboration model allows participants to share knowledge almost completely free of the cultural and interpersonal barriers described in Chapters 8, 9, and 10.

With slight modifications, the virtual collaboration scenario can easily be migrated back into traditional conference room settings. The only technology dependency that falls out in such a translation is the reference to tweets and re-tweets. Of course there's ample room for speculation about social media technologies providing similar value in the workplace,[154] but I believe it's an area that will see considerable innovation ahead. Stay tuned for some breakthroughs here in the next few years.

Scenario 3: Formal Approach.
Physical—Adaptive Model

A more formalized process is critical for larger groups, more complex problems, long-running serial sessions, or scenarios where high-quality alternatives can't be left to chance. In terms of which roles perform which process steps, I've provided managers with a familiar but basic RACI Diagram in FIGURE 23 to show how the ownership of the various roles is usually spread across the team. "RACI" is an acronym for the 4 types of commitment categories defined for this model (see legend of FIGURE 23 for specifics), defining levels of engagement for each role defined in that specific analysis. For this diagram, I grouped some of the key roles defined in Chapter 14. I've also added to the RACI an assessment of where the risk of failure is the highest, summarizing takeaways from the detailed process descriptions earlier in this chapter.

Process RACI Commitment Levels for each Collaboration Step	Moderator	Group	Aggregator	Risk Due to Difficulty
1-Framing	A	R	R,C,I	HIGH
2-Introductions & Guidelines	A	R	R	Low
3-Setting & Holding Context	A	R	R,C,I	HIGH
4-Brainstorming via Dialogue	R	A	R	Moderate
5-Identifying Patterns	R	A	R	HIGH
6-Synthesis	R	R	A	HIGH

"A"=Accountable - the moderator owns Framing & Context throughout the collaboration, while the group members own Brainstorming and Pattern Identification, the steps where content is generated and prioritized. The Aggregator is on the hook for the synthesis phase, though this role must remain engaged and visible throughout.

"R"=Responsible designation implies these roles are actively engaged on each task; they are essentially doing the work.

"C"=Consulting and "I"=Inform categories show which roles continue to participate in the background and to sustain awareness throughout the process flow. Note these statuses don't appear much in this RACI, due to high levels of engagement.

FIGURE 23 – "Who Owns What?"
Relationships among key activity streams and roles

So what might be gathered here? One implication is that the group contributors must be heavily engaged throughout. Another is that the moderator is most busy in the beginning of the session; the aggregator, in contrast, toward the end. Many collaboration sessions do not have an aggregator, but I've seen a decline in the quantity and quality of outcomes when this role is shared, split, or neglected outright. The capture of takeaways is absolutely essential for intentional collaboration to produce a usable result.

Capturing Takeaways:
Requirements for Work Space

Over and over, I've emphasized the importance of capturing the results of our collaborative efforts. The quality of our work at this step is critical to the quality of collaborative outcomes.

Collaboration Workspace Requirement	Current Platform	Typical Advantages	Current Limitations
Achieving an Accessible, Integrated Workspace Allowing for threaded and non-threaded conversation, comment/response, document storage and graphic annotation Space a key requirement Should integrate well with other desktop & messaging tools	**Wikis**	Ease of initial capture	Mark-up a barrier Limited conversation
	Blogs	Space Threaded conversation Feedback management	Limited document management
	Status Apps	Conversational Spontaneity	Limited document management
	Presence Apps	Accessible Conversational	Limited space
	Cloud-based Workspaces	Accessible	Limited functionality (early stage evolution)
	Document Repositories	Accessible Workflow	Limited conversation
	Email Systems	Ubiquitous Intuitive	Lack of threading Version control Search limitations

FIGURE 24 – Collaborative Workspace Requirements
Considerations for supporting Technology Platforms to unlock Collaboration DNA

This is the point in the process where value is typically left on the table, sometimes literally. This begs an important question: where should all these takeaways go?

At a minimum, our collaborative outputs must be captured electronically. Flip charts and white boards can be a great source of white space in the conventional way it's known—a place to write things down—but they are also apt to be lost when the next group enters the conference room. We need electronic notes captured, including a means for review and distribution, one that is preferably *not* email. Ideally, notes can be captured in a threaded manner, so one comment may be built upon the next.

The feedback process should be iterative.

I believe we will see explosive innovation in collaborative workspaces over the next few years. There are a several software vendors in the market today who are producing early solutions to this problem, but none have deployed solutions that fully grasp the requirements of a functioning, high-energy collaborative team.

In FIGURE 24, I've provided a recap of core requirements as I see them, based on the Collaboration DNA approach. There are two challenges in the social technology market today:

- **Vendor Proliferation.** No one vendor has secured a leadership position, and the barriers to competitive entry (at least in the open internet market) remain relatively low. This has led to the current state of vendor proliferation and the overwhelming number of choices that early adopters of social technology must navigate.

- **Feature Wars.** As a result of the saturation of vendors, each is vying to gain a richer feature set, so the capabilities of software solutions are changing at a breakneck pace. Both factors serve to confuse customers and delay adoption, which is already longer than most would prefer.[155] The impact on the enterprise collaboration market has yet to fully resolve, but I see change on the horizon.

TAKEAWAYS for "Process"

With an experienced collaboration team the emergence of insights and ideas are rapid and sometimes even immediate, regardless of venue or process. With practice, intentional collaborators can begin to solve problems more quickly and efficiently, relying less and less on supporting processes. The magic is truly in the exchange, the energy brought by contributors, and the dynamics that emerge from their interaction. What can we do to help accelerate the learning effort that might lead to this level of expertise?

- **T1. After collaborating using the process outlined here, try collaborating without it; can you see the difference?**

- **T2. Try collaborating with very small, mid-size, and then larger groups, and watch how the dynamics shift; do you see the need for process increasing with group size?**

- **T3. Try virtual collaboration, if you haven't; it's fascinating, powerful and educational.**

Experienced collaborators will rely less on space and process. Until we get there, the process outline here is useful as a scaffolding to help us get started. Don't be constrained by it. Challenge it. Change it. But in the organizational setting, don't turn your back on it—at least, not until everyone is ready.

17 – Balanced Objectives

Solving difficult problems requires an ability to focus. This is core to critical thinking. Do we understand the current situation? Can we frame alternative solution scenarios? If it sounds easy, be careful. Establishing and sustaining a common view of the end objectives can be elusive when people collaborate. The same energy that generates a considerable stockpile of insights and ideas will also create numerous tangents and conversational rabbit trails, leading the group away from its ultimate objectives.

Creative energy and idea synthesis require time, space, and room to experiment. Short periods of chaotic drift can be valuable. Sometimes longer running tangents prove fruitful. There is no set formula. But ultimately, for collaboration to produce results, the group must gain discipline in bringing the open-ended brainstorm back to a focused end point.

This is an area where the delicate balance between structure and chaos is, over the long run, a make-or-break differentiator. Groups that get this right produce results. Those that don't will come up short.

To establish an overall framework for the free space required for brainstorming (where an objective remains in sight but detours are allowed), I've found the most effective approach is a clear framing statement for the session, along these lines: *"The goal of this exchange is to explore factors that contribute to X."* From this, much can happen: sharing numerous raw insights, partial or fully developed ideas, the injection of new, alternative contexts, and even some early synthesis of thinking. It may sometimes seem like the overarching objective is lost, when in fact it's only suspended for a short time. The overarching focus can be easily recovered. Over the life of a more complex collaboration, the brainstorming in early stages will be much more loose and open-ended, with less demand for circling back to state objectives.

Generation of insights early in the process calls for more freedom and more space. Later, when options have begun to crystallize and less-productive rabbit trails become more obvious, the level of focus and bias for keeping to objectives goes up.

Even the framing statements tighten up, perhaps along the lines of: *"The goal of this session is to refine solution Y and eliminate open issues and ambiguities in scenarios A, B and C."*

The balancing point shifts in favor of more precision as the collaboration advances. A useful metaphor for the discovery process wraps around the balanced dynamic of *explore* (early, open-ended, divergent thinking) vs. *exploit* (later, more focused discovery, convergent thinking). You'll recall we discussed this distinction earlier, in Chapter 3 on Outcomes (see FIGURE 6, p. 50). Now we seek to balance these opposing analytical strategies.

Imagine early American pioneers making a journey across country, facing decisions whether to keep exploring or to settle down on a given spot and build a new home. Framed as a metaphor, we might say:

M21. Collaboration is exploration.

Our journey is intended to *discover* new spaces.[156]
We'll continue to *search* for a suitable place to settle.
For a complex problem, many barriers must be *traversed.*

Then, once we believe we're onto something tangible:

M22. Collaboration is exploitation.
When I find a solution, I'll put *stakes in the ground*.
We will *harvest* the fruit of our labor when this
research is completed.
Our approach produced a *gold mine* of opportunity.

How do we know when to stop exploring, and start exploiting our new ideas? That's the ultimate judgment call, because there's no right answer. It requires a balancing act. Leaders must watch for a critical mass of thinking, maybe even a tipping point, representing an opportunity for the group to move more in depth to focus on a viable solution. Over time, senior group members, as they become expert collaborators, can assist in becoming vigilant. When exploring the frontier, settlers had to wear many hats. With experience, collaborators learn patterns that represent increasing levels of opportunity, and avoid the trap of taking a formulaic approach.

The split decision to explore or exploit comes up in the study of complexity, which we'll touch on soon.

Collaborative interaction should be loosely guided by a set of principles for engagement, guidelines that can maximize productivity and minimize the friction associated with differences of approach, mindset, and communication skills. The level of oversight is a delicate balance. Within that delicate balance, however, a set of simple principles provides important boundaries. Think of them as "bumpers" like the ones on pool tables, to keep balls in play.[157]

M23. Collaboration is like a Game of Billiards.
The framework helped him *deflect* his thinking from
going *out of bounds*.
Our ideas *bounced* around in a rapid, chaotic way.
His aim well but *missed the mark* on execution.

I've provided some guidelines in FIGURE 25 that I've used in successful collaboration sessions. These are by no means definitive, but they can serve as a foundation.

Sample Collaboration Guidelines

1. **Objectives.** The group agrees to specific goal(s) of the collaboration, and agrees to apply reasonable focus, energy and good faith efforts to achieve such ends.
2. **Moderation.** The group acknowledges the coordination role of the group moderator, and will make reasonable efforts to abide by recommendations provided during the collaboration, in the interest of achieving collaboration objectives.
3. **Respect.** All contributors agree to regard others in the group with respect and will conduct interactions in a professional manner; at no time should comments be of a negative personal nature.
4. **Brevity.** Contributors agree to limit the length and frequency of their contributions so that they remain in line with other contributors, subject to specific exceptions per moderator guidance.
5. **Conflicts.** All individual differences should be resolved offline from the collaboration, to respect time of others.
6. **Creative Commons.** Generally, unless otherwise specified in advance, the comments, insights, ideas and proposed solutions shared by each contributor in public are assumed to fall under the creative commons, meaning they are intended for public consumption and non-commercial reuse.
7. **Intellectual Property.** Some contributors, by virtue of their employment, may be subject to intellectual property ("IP") constraints to protect confidential company information about which they may be aware. Each contributor is expected to understand the full scope, force and domain of these limitations, and to retain full responsibility for non-disclosure of any corporate IP that may enter into the commons by virtue of their participation.

FIGURE 25 – Collaboration Guidelines (Sample)
Sample ground rules for group interaction

At least one Organizational Development specialist of note, Patricia Shaw, seems generally opposed to excessive use of ground rules and structure[158] and from the open, organic perspective of complexity I see her point. But I also think a balanced, adaptive approach to ground rules—again, using the bumper metaphor—can provide structure and flow, without sacrificing open space.

Within these guidelines is mention of one of the largest challenges facing collaborators in the commercial domain: the notion of intellectual property (see FIGURE 25, Guidelines 6 and 7). In the U.S. at least, it's the legal underpinning of all copyrights, patents, and trademarks, and the basis for how many companies sustain competitive leadership in the marketplace. At the extreme risk of oversimplifying a fairly complex set of laws, if an individual or company can prove they're first to market with a unique concept, invention, or commercially-viable idea, the law protects their ability to make money from it. This commercial construct has spawned a deeply protective view of great ideas. R&D departments have traditionally lurked in the shadows behind locked doors, so that breakthrough product ideas can't leak to the competition, though companies like Google, 3M, Nike, and Apple have found ways to navigate these rapids using both traditional and creative approaches.[159]

Groups will want to adapt these guidelines for their purposes, but again, consistent with the idea of Adaptive Governance, these should remain guidelines and not become hard and fast rules.

What About Data?

When we collaborate, we must often use concrete data to support our ideas. We might want to leverage facts, figures, compiled insights, charts, survey results, tables, graphs, infographics, database extracts, and reports of every variety. In a fairly real-world sense, knowledge knows few bounds, and data is our proof. In fact, we could bring so much data to our meetings that we could pile it high enough to obscure the faces across the table. No surprise that in some collaborative exchanges, this has actually been attempted. We need to pause and ask: how much data is realistic? What are we trying to accomplish by bringing it into focus?

Ultimately, to reach a viable solution, our arguments will need support. Facts, figures, and data must enter the fray somehow, because ignoring data runs the risk of faulty arguments or pure, unsupported speculation.

Clearly, it is yet another balancing act.

For real-time collaboration, we'll stay focused primarily on the qualitative, non-numeric aspects, driven and informed by data, but not hard-wired to it. The driver here is one of practicality, limited by what can be easily exchanged via conversation. Data can block flow of insight and we need to ensure that this flow is not broken. Supporting quantitative data can and should be shared and analyzed offline, with results or key points brought forward into the conversation. Solution teams will need to allocate offline time to test proposals that collaborators have introduced. But I've found obsession with data in real-time conversations can derail a productive exchange. I believe that sometimes this is by design. Data is a good thing, but not when it's used as a weapon.

Our Western world is steeped in process. For me, the move from structure to flow will be critically important, and it will challenge almost every notion of process that we bring to the table. The light-weight process offered here in Part 4 is my best effort at compromise, in that it seeks to offer a blend of the demands levied by the competing camps. I am greatly encouraged because I have been using the process outlined in Chapter 16, FIGURE 21, for 3 years, serving as our standard discussion model for both the #SMCHAT and #ECOSYS Twitter communities. I know it works, because we've used it with success every week since April 2009. Among the group's leaders, we think of it as *innovation on the ground*, a step-wise approach to expand the possibilities of virtual collaboration.

No doubt there is room for improvement.

But as a starting point, I offer it with the clear conscience of a project manager who has learned to turn find the "off-switch" for structure and control. I didn't say it was easy. But it can be done.

TAKEAWAYS for "Balance"

What is the ideal balance between affinity and diversity? How do we know when it's time to expand possibilities with new ideas, vs. trying to exploit the ones we've already discovered? These are judgment calls, where the group gets to experiment and find out what works. Sharpen your skills in this area by challenging your assumptions:

- **T1. How diverse should a group be to cover the necessary dimensions of the problem, but without being so diverse as to find no common ground? How can you manage this?**

- **T2. How much similarity or affinity can you afford before the group begins to engage in *group think*?**

- **T3. Does the concept of *adaptive governance* resonate with you? Have you seen it in action? Can you imagine how it would work?**

This is an area where prescriptive "right or wrong" answers don't apply. Be creative, and again, let your judgment be your guide.

PART 5: POSSIBILITIES

"The future belongs to those who see possibilities before they become obvious."

John Scully

18 – Are We Ready?

In *The DNA of Collaboration* we've explored the many dimensions of team-based problem-solving, and we've done it piece by piece. We've discussed barriers, enablers, core skills and adoption challenges. We've looked at process scenarios and explored key tools. Without a doubt we've covered considerable ground. Now it's time to reflect on our potential to move ahead.

Are we ready to collaborate?

How will we know?

I've been careful to avoid a checklist approach in this book for several reasons. A checklist encourages a shortcut mentality, validating the misnomer that silver bullets are out there if only we could find them. It also perpetuates a mindset that our skill development has a binary nature: if we can check the box, we've done everything that needs to be done, ignoring the reality that our learning and problem solving skills lie on a continuum. There are no high stakes tests to tell us when we've passed to the next level, and there will always room for improvement. Checklists are especially problematic when the subject matter is qualitative, with scope and scale open for discussion, ever subject to fuzzy boundaries. As my friend and colleague Gregg Powers would say, for all matters subjective and analytical: "reasonable minds will disagree."

But we can still put stakes in the ground, and there's value in doing so. Collaborating teams face difficulties when they forge into unchartered territory, which is, not ironically, their sweet spot. Solving wicked problems is likely the place where they can add the most value. Thumbing back through these pages should leave no doubt as to the complexity of the challenges that team-based problem solving represents. Setting the difficult problems and subject matter aside, simply coming together and staying together with a unified intent is a significant challenge, in and of itself.

Collaborating teams need to get (and keep) their bearings.

For teams that wish to excel, the ability to track progress against clearly articulated goals will always be on the critical path, reinforcing critical momentum through short-term wins.[160] Such teams need to become plainly aware of their capabilities, to understand gaps so they can develop plans to mitigate them, to set expectations for what can be accomplished and to openly discuss areas for improvement.

At the end of Chapter 4 on Intention, I introduced a simple framework for tracking our readiness, using an 8-vector capability model. Each category (shown as a vector, emanating from the center) represents progress on a major dimension of Collaboration DNA. The outermost edge of the circle represents achievement of 100%, the ultimate goal; it's a simple charting method that can be used to track progress across many categories of capabilities at once.[161]

Tracking progress with a model like this is easy, because drawing the picture and proposing data points can stimulate discussion quickly. The diagram is tailor-made for reproducing on a white board. Group members can weigh-in interactively quickly and informally, until consensus is reached.

What would such graphs look like when filled in?

With the caveat that teams can redefine the vectors to meet their preferences, I'll stay with the 8-vector framework from Chapter 4 and provide three sample readiness "read-outs" to show the model in use.

Scenario 1: Formative Potential (FIGURE 26). This situation shows a team that is relatively new. Such a group has likely

FIGURE 26 – Formative (Getting Started)
Initial focus areas for new Collaborative Teams

met only recently, and has yet to establish working relationships. Communication skills may be in place for some, but the ability to tap those skills across the team broader team isn't there yet. FOCUS: A primary goal is to start working on **[1] Respect and Trust**, which can be sparked by a simple exchange of each member's interests and capabilities. Also in these early stages, efforts to build **[2] Improved Semantics** and **Communication Skills** is helpful; getting people talking helps establish common ground. Focus on problem definitions is good practice, but it helps to spend just a bit of time on process and ground rules. This helps us advance progress in the direction of the engagement competency, shown by the white arrow as a secondary benefit.

Scenario 2: Moderate Team Potential (FIGURE 27). After working together for some time, our hypothetical team will probably have shown improvement in many dimensions, getting points across in both concrete and abstract contexts.

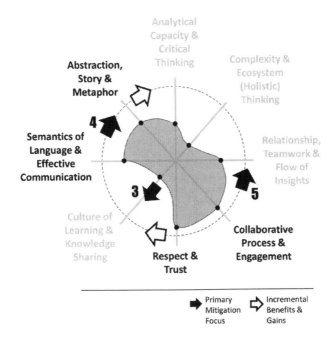

FIGURE 27 – Moderate Potential, Ready to Collaborate
Improvement areas shift as the group matures, gaining
competency in several areas

The team will start to move their "progress points" (black dots) further out, to reflect team capability closer to the 100% target band. FOCUS: **[3] Culture** changes only slowly, so progress there is expected to take a while, but it's an area to keep in focus; a highly effective collaborative group can be a catalyst for cultural improvement, becoming a case study for what is possible, with its members serving as collaboration role models. With a stronger foundation in **[4] Advanced Communication skills** it's possible to tackle more challenging problems, working to navigate changes in abstraction. This increases the group's ability to change context fluidly, working toward new levels of critical thinking (white arrow). These skills allow the group to attack more holistic issues with even more domain cross-over. **[5] Relationships** among the team are continuing to improve, and some friendships are forming.

Scenario 3, Mature (FIGURE 28). A mature team has overcome issues of culture, semantics, and abstraction, though culture will always be an improvement area (white arrow).

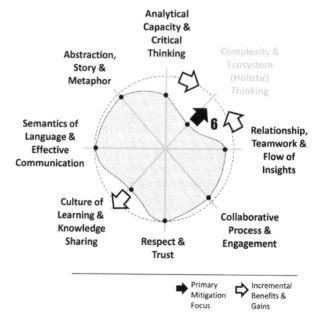

FIGURE 28 – Highest Team Potential, Mature
Now well-rounded (literally!) the group has advanced in each major competency, and is ready to tackle the toughest problems

The level of trust is now very strong, except for some minor professional differences, though personal issues are quickly worked out offline because relationships are strong throughout the team. The group can apply critical thinking with increased ease and speed, having learned the traps and pitfalls that tend to shortcut analytical rigor. FOCUS: The most difficult problems are within reach now, where **[6] Complexity and Ecosystem Thinking** challenges everyone to stay focused and on top of many dynamics in play at once. The mature collaborative team is ready to tackle the toughest problems.

Let's cover some final thoughts to wrap this up.

Calling out individuals must be avoided in the rating process, along with a tendency to get consumed with numerical scoring. Progress towards 100% is relative, and requires only general consensus. Agree on data points quickly, and move on.

For long-running collaborations, revisiting progress monthly or quarterly helps the group understand and appreciate headway; while the outer "ring" drawn at 100% is used to target long-term goals, a secondary "inner ring" for near-term objectives may be useful. This gives the group a way to conceptualize and envision needed progress. If the group is struggling, creating some interim goals helps focus on near-term wins.

The specific definitions for each dimension (or vector) of readiness can be shifted without penalty, to track progress in any direction the team wishes to track. Here, I've consolidated eight critical competencies that emerged for me as I wrote and then reflected upon *The DNA of Collaboration*.

TAKEAWAYS for "Readiness"

A newly formed collaboration team should go through the baseline-setting process as a team building exercise, as an early part of the collaborative process. Sharing insights and responding to those of others is excellent practice. Here are some more areas for focus, and things to try.

- **T1. What about buy-in? Some may love this visual model and others will not, reflecting the highly diverse nature of how people think. The best course is not to spend too much time here. Use 15 to 20 minutes up-front to establish an initial baseline, and then use a brief 5-minute check-in at the end of sessions to monitor progress.**

- **T2. If evaluating a specific category is proving difficult, create an Ishikawa diagram for it; this allows the group to list out, categorize and prioritize contributing factors; with key factors identified, a targeted mitigation plan can be constructed.**

- **T3. What do you think are the toughest dimensions to master?**

- **T4. If the group is having trouble envisioning what 100% success for a given category looks like, challenge team members with an offline assignment to create a goal statement for it, using the descriptions in this chapter as examples. Have participants report back to the group.**

Measuring progress should never become an obsession or primary focus. It should be a key supporting activity over the long term. If the team believes it adds value, it's clearly worth a small investment of thought, time and effort.

19 – The Evolution of Knowledge Management

Knowledge sharing, as it turns out, isn't all that easy. By now, the reasons why should be clear. Throughout the book we've been discussing the challenge of capturing our abstract and complex ideas in useful ways, seeking mechanisms that help us describe our thoughts to others. We've looked at the nuances of language, the use of metaphor, and even simple visual frameworks. These are all tools that help us build the conceptual scaffolding of ideas under construction, giving us approaches to explain our thinking, on the path to effective collaboration.

That's the base case, the foundation we seek.

Can all this work in the modern enterprise?

Imagine how quickly we compound the problem when we try to perform these capabilities within and across the deep functional silos of a large organization. We are instantly flooded with barriers, with more resistance and more inertia than perhaps we'd considered.

Advancement of organizational learning and broad scale collaboration has, in fact, been attempted. For almost two decades, the practice of Knowledge Management ("KM") has been focused on tackling these and similar problems. What is clearly challenging to most small collaborative teams becomes exponentially more difficult when scale and increased complexity are introduced. There is little more complex than the organizational dynamics of the modern commercial organization. Academic, public sector and social ecosystems share similar profiles. We shouldn't be surprised that KM has struggled.

During KM's first two decades there have been valiant efforts and several successes.[162] Some businesses such as professional consulting firms are so riddled with proprietary knowledge (or *intellectual property*) that KM emerged early on as a vital competency for those segments. But in mainstream commercial spaces, KM has faced more resistance. Some of it has been cultural, reflecting a resistance to knowledge sharing, as we covered in Chapter 10. But I believe the challenges are more endemic to the KM process itself. In short, like the rest of our industrialized Western culture, I believe KM has been working from the wrong metaphor.

KM must be less about structure and more about flow.

When a prevailing paradigm in use by a group of practitioners shows structural cracks, I like to go back to the founding fathers for that space, to see what guidance we may have missed, what may have changed in our environment, or to see where we may have run off the rails along the way.

The path for KM leads us quickly back to Nonaka, a highly respected thought leader and one of KM's most outspoken visionaries. His "SECI" model is a cycle that traces the conversion of knowledge from tacit/unspoken form to the explicit/written artifact, and back again. It's a hallmark vision that describes how knowledge changes *state*, so to speak; a analogy would be changing from ice to water, then back to ice.

This is what most KM practitioners know about Nonaka.

But Nonaka also advocated three themes in his foundational work that have more relevance today than ever. Each of them still brings important dynamics of KM into view, and I believe each deserves renewed attention in the 21st Century organizational context:

- **Flow of Insights.** The most fundamental change in the KM paradigm must be moving from *structure* to *flow* as the prevailing metaphor. Insights flow through an organization. They don't live in hierarchical boxes. Nonaka's SECI model is a cycle that *looks like* a flow, but it's not in the broader, more macro-level sense of flow through an organization. KM must address macro-level, enterprise-wide flow as well, where knowledge moves among stakeholders, including flow across silos and across the firewall. Social networks are a better model for how insight truly flows in an organization, representing a key inflection point for what is possible that is only now becoming a viable option in the modern enterprise.[163]

- **Pursuing *Ba* = A Collaboration Opportunity (in practice).** In Japanese, *ba* translates to "time and space" but in the practice of KM it is used to represent an opportunity for collaboration to happen. It could be a conference room, an office, or space by the water cooler that allows for periodic exchange. In the modern context these spaces can also be virtual. Regardless of the place, when ideas begin to flow there needs to be a way to capture, store, and review what is generated. Water coolers aren't good for that, but as we covered in Chapter 13, social technologies are excellent at allowing the emergence of *ba* in virtual settings.

- **Taking Time to Care.** Sadly, many people and their companies have lost sight of what they really care about, in the context of *core values*. In cases where they ARE stated, they often fail to enter into the day-to-day reality. Nonaka has excellent insight on why ownership and compassion make a difference in KM, and we need to get back in touch with it.

All of these are important elements of a viable KM program, and none of them have been successfully implemented to date. To understand KM deeply and seek new solutions to unsolved problems, we need to look beyond SECI and read the rest of Nonaka.[164]

KM in the Business Context

Peter Drucker offered us some insight in this space back in 1988, even before KM began to be called KM. Perhaps that's why we missed it. The basic idea is that the earliest historical corporate conglomerates (dating from the early 20th Century) were managed *exclusively* from the top-down; all the knowledge was held at the top, and by his account, everyone else was basically a helper. Drucker predicted that in the future, all the truly important knowledge would be held at the bottom of the company, a trend that appears to have come to pass.[165] Looking around, I'd say his prediction was spot on. Yet across industry, the majority of companies continue to be organized and run as if the knowledge were held by a select few at the top. It's a 1920's model, one that predates the Information Age by decades.

Drucker as we now know seldom (if ever) got it wrong.

I think this is yet another fundamental mandate for KM to reinvent itself. We need to foster the flow of insights up and through our organizations, placing a premium on insights generated at the edges of the company, whether from its customers, it's functional knowledge workers, or on the shop floor. Awareness of change and opportunity can best be found at an organization's boundaries. The alternative, relying on a top-down flow of insights—or more accurately, instructions—represents an incredibly dated model, one that's out of touch with the realities of a knowledge economy.

To drive home the business imperative, there is yet another strong voice to consider: the perspectives of Thomas Stewart. His *Wealth of Knowledge* (2001) is a profoundly practical guidebook for KM in the business context. As a former editor at *Harvard Business Review* and *Fortune*, he's had the catbird's seat to watch patterns evolve across the commercial landscape. Let's highlight several of Stewart's most important perspectives:

> *The value of ideas isn't taught in traditional economics; it's treated as a mysterious, outside force.*

> *A company in the information age is really a beehive of ideas, impacting how they should be set up and run, and how they should compete.*

> *Forward-thinking companies realize their future competitiveness will be in their ideas.*[166]

An evolved, future-state KM needs more grounding in business and the business process in the contextual frame that Stewart provides. Think about the concept of **work flow**, and many examples will come to mind. KM needs to be embedded in daily operations, and the sharing of insights must become second nature.

One of the failings of KM has been an obsession with structure and categorization. But knowledge is too fluid to fit into the hierarchical boxes into which we've been trying to force it. It would be unfair to levy this burden on KM practitioners alone, however, because KM has been subject to the same prevailing organizational metaphors as the rest of the business community. The Factory Metaphor (M14) has deeply reinforced notions of hierarchy and control in all aspects of our culture, reflected in how corporations are organized and how information tends to move, if it moves at all: up and down hierarchies. In this context, we could argue that KM has been trying to solve the problem in the manner it was framed by the business world. This, to me, is more than an academic conclusion. It's strong evidence that the entire KM undertaking has suffered from the same structural constraints as its customers, its vendors, and its purveyors at-large. The problem is cultural, and it's embedded in our mental models of how business was believed to work best over 100 years ago.

Rather than attempting to "blow up" KM or otherwise pursue its demise, as many frustrated practitioners and CIOs advocate, I believe KM is an ideal candidate for a collaborative redesign at the industry level. What we need to attack is our dysfunctional mindset, the thinking that's filled with dated mental models that effectively block innovation. With the old models, we are literally unable to see what the future holds.

Technology Adoption
(KM and Social Networks)

In his 2009 book *Enterprise 2.0*, Andrew McAfee sets a new baseline for what's possible with social technology in the modern organization. Many embraced his vision fairly quickly, as it represented a useful and appealing view of our future. McAfee put a finer point on the foundational thinking of Friedman, O'Reilly and Tapscott, all of them advancing the cause in relevant and important ways. Unfortunately, in the years since *Enterprise 2.0,* the practice and implementation of KM and related technologies have made few of the necessary inroads.

McAfee cites research that paints a slow road ahead for the adoption of social technologies, along with broad-scale technology adoption in general.[167]

While I agree with his forecast and its plodding trajectory, in this case I think much of the delay is rooted in the old paradigm of structure and hierarchy. Like the factory model itself, it's a paradigm that's deeply engrained in how we think about the enterprise and the manner in which information needs to flow through it. In the old world we relied exclusively on databases and reports. In the new world, unstructured conversations become important sources of innovation, as well.

It's a big leap for CIOs, but a critical leap all the same.

Framing KM as a new paradigm allows us all to rethink what might happen when insight truly begins to flow more freely across organizational boundaries. After all, recalling the DNA at collaboration's core, insights are the raw material of new ideas. Knowledge is the outcome. If we go all the way back to our River Leaves Metaphor (M2) we can gain some sense of what *flow* truly means. The river is dynamic and fluid, interrupted from time to time with obstacles that change its course, following an ever-changing path. In this space, there's a constant risk we'll miss something flowing past us.

This is the nature of conversation, and the flow of ideas.

And this is the promise of social technologies.

Technology adoption in the enterprise always demands some basic rationalization, of course. A CIO can't rely on metaphorical explanations to explain the ROI (or return on investment) for the next key KM investment, but metaphor can open the conversation. What is the benefit of KM? Why should we invest time and money here? To address this effectively, we need to articulate approaches that will resonate with C-levels, in the form of a viable semantic frame; *social media* doesn't pass muster, and neither does *knowledge management*. We need to capture the objectives in the context of everyday business challenges. I've increasingly seen traction with the simple concept of "getting smarter, faster" as well as describing the value of "the connected organization." These frames require little explanation. They both get straight to the point. Recalling Chapter 5, when seeking deep changes, the semantics are critical. Far too often, on matters like these, we repeatedly miss the boat. In a real sense, the CEO, CFO, and CIO having conversations like this are attempting to collaborate. As a team, how can they crack the curse of gridlock? Let's outline the highlights of such a conversation.

An Executive Discussion on "Flow of Insight"

Frame: *How much is it worth for the organization to get smarter, faster?*

Participants: CEO, CFO and CIO.

Talking Points: There should be some tangible value. Let's have a look at the status quo, to evaluate current pain points. What are the broader implications (both strategic and financial) if people across the organization *aren't* getting smarter at an increased rate? Could key projects be delayed? Will aggressive goals not be reached? Will innovation imperatives remain stranded? Are great ideas stuck in organizational silos?

Insights: If the CEO and CFO are listening (perhaps flipping back to Chapter 8 for a refresher) the group could launch into a useful and important discussion about the value of emerging ideas, productivity, talent development, and the need for the organization to expand its core problem-solving competencies. And what about social technology; couldn't it help us?

Actions: Roadmaps are drafted, pilots are funded, and collaboration tools begin to appear.

Of course technology sometimes carries a hefty price tag. CIOs and their suppliers must find ways to make the flow of knowledge affordable and ubiquitous. John Hagel, for one, believes the business case for IT investments in this space could be compelling.[168]

Fortunately, the technologies I've described in Part 4 cost a fraction of traditional enterprise ERP and CRM solutions. Some of these very same vendors are beginning to embed collaboration tools in their core offerings as well, a good trend for the accelerated adoption of social technologies.[169] And there's even more upside here: everyone across the organization can gradually become less reliant on their email to get work done, shifting to more productive ways to interact. That's good news for everybody, especially C-Levels.

Of course, the circumstances of your own organization will vary to an extent. The context of your company must be factored in carefully, to ensure you're not trying to solve a specific problem with a generalized solution.

But I see progress here, some value in a new way to attack some long-term problems. As we attack the framing, the semantic messaging, and the possible platforms for delivery, we're starting to reframe the promise of KM in more practical terms. We've giving it a value equation with a stronger foundation.

Yet something is still missing from our story. What is the value proposition for our people?

Human Factors

I think a powerful accelerator for a revitalized KM is to introduce the concept of the *connected organization*. In this model, people come together to collaborate who were only recently strangers. It brings *serendipity* to the KM value proposition, an aspect missing from the structured approach.[170] It's what we've been discussing throughout the book, an approach that fosters the exchange of insight among diverse stakeholders and diverse teams, creating new and creative ways to drive innovation.

Connections between an organization's stakeholders happen at many levels, often spontaneously and in the moment. Email is not effective for this. Encounters at the water cooler leave too much to chance.

Humans as social creatures have an innate desire to connect[171] but that thinking hasn't gone far in our commercial spaces. My take is that corporations, in general, have failed to recognize the tremendous generative power in fostering white space and open linkages. To me, it's time to take a confident step in the direction of Enterprise 2.0. Social technologies offer the potential to serve as a KM catalyst, helping people connect in intuitive ways, when the need becomes apparent.

As I explored the ideas that now comprise the conceptual scaffolding in *The DNA of Collaboration,* I've begun to appreciate the deep linkage between KM and the collaboration process, and the role that technology can play to transcend historic barriers. Both KM and collaboration depend on the exchange of insight, both aspire to create synergy from the engagement of independent thinkers, and both struggle to function across organizational silos. Some say KM and collaboration are the same thing and Peter Senge would agree, describing KM and collaboration as two sides of the same coin.[172]

KM needs to traffic in the flow of insight, building formal and informal knowledge networks as linkage mechanism for newly (or increasingly) connected organizations. These new networks, leveraging social technology **on both sides of the firewall** become catalysts for collaboration, leveraging virtual or physical *ba* (as available), and finding places to turn insights into ideas, and then solutions. That, in the end, is how innovation happens. The magic of a connected organization is to spark new capabilities that weren't present before, and to do so in a highly organic and intuitive way.

In the process, several important things happen:

- **Stakeholders opt in to participate in the knowledge network**
- **Connections are organically identified and established by stakeholders**
- **Ubiquitous tagging is enabled across the organization to establish and maintain context as it evolves**
- **Insights are exchanged and expanded into ideas and solutions, using collaborative process models and tools outlined in *The DNA of Collaboration***
- **An organic knowledge base evolves**
- **Relevance is established via active content interaction and metadata tags, which fundamentally enhances search**
- **Structure gives way to flow, modeling a new paradigm for enterprise collaboration**

The task ahead in Knowledge Management is nothing short of transformation. It's about rethinking the work group. It's about erasing artificial boundaries.

It's about opening our minds to change.

As a KM practitioner, I find many aren't ready to cross that threshold. The prevailing paradigm of "how things are supposed to work" in hierarchical boxes remains strong. After all, KM is modeled on a business architecture that is 100 years old. But more and more people I talk to are ready to try a different approach, and I count myself among them.[173] KM is not alone in reinventing itself. As Kuhn taught us 50 years ago, practitioners in every space must be alert for shifting paradigms, when old solutions don't seem to fit new problems.[174] It's the stuff of change—never easy, but always the path to breakthrough thinking.

TAKEAWAYS for "KM"

Reflecting on the flow of insights through an organization will be new for the vast majority of us, because it is an approach that has seldom been achieved. Let's imagine the possibilities as we tackle these questions:

- **T1. How many of the vectors in Chapter 18's Readiness Framework apply in the pursuit of knowledge sharing? Better still, are there any that do *not* apply?**

- **T2. In your own experience, what cultural barriers constrain the exchange of insights across organizational silos, and what can be done to mitigate them?**

- **T3. Sketch the path of a new idea that comes in through your organization's customer service department; or, if you're in the role of customer, trace an idea of your own that you've phoned in to a company. How far can it travel? Does it bounce up and down hierarchies? Or does it flow to where it needs to flow?**

- **T4. What industries are most likely to embrace the flow of insights, and why?**

- **T5. Why does an organization that cares about its people and customers have a different view of knowledge than one focused on its own self-serving ends?**

Knowledge management has yet to come to terms with its future. Questions like these may begin to define new pathways.

Are you an advocate for the flow of insights?

If so, you may be just the catalyst for change that your organization has been seeking.

20 – Critical Thinking

A Path to Understanding

Experts will debate how to define it, but I believe the ability to think critically is a fundamental competency for collaborators, and a central theme in *the DNA of Collaboration*.

We've defined critical thinking as the ability to *perform deep and thorough analysis on the many dimensions of a problem.* You'll recall we delved deeper in Chapter 2 to explore the foundations of this. Remember our power tools? It's about challenging surface appearances. It's about navigating abstraction, and dealing with ambiguity. It's about learning to set and hold context, changing scenarios as required. It's about understanding root cause. It's about learning to develop simple framework for our ideas, so that we might share them with others so they might be made better. It all requires mindful awareness, tapping knowledge of our own cognitive filters and guarding against subtle mental heuristics and emotions that trigger when we least expect them to.

Embracing definitions like these clearly raises the bar for all of us. The level of thinking skills required is deeper than required for daily life. We must bring new levels of rigor to how we approach everything we do.

Throughout the book, we've been discussing the many dimensions that impact team-based critical thinking. Some of these require specific cognitive skills, like the ones described above. But in other sections we addressed still more factors influencing our success. We've looked at messaging and intention; barriers and enablers that arise in our relationships; processes that provide space, with an emphasis on flow and iteration. All of these foundational aspects must be mastered (classic Senge)[175] to even contemplate the rigor of critical thinking in a collaborative setting.

The progressive stepping stones of human learning are well-documented in both widely published versions of Bloom's *Learning Taxonomy*.[176] Understanding the structured elements of learning can only help us embrace the many aspects of discovery that critical thinking requires. Let's look at Bloom in the collaboration context:

Learning Dimensions from *Bloom/Anderson Taxonomy*		Collaboration Impact
Remember	Ability to recall facts	*Foundational*
Understand	Ability to construct meaning	*Foundational* – but a key area for focus in collaboration; a deep understanding can be difficult as groups move to more advanced, complex topics; ability to use language, metaphor and story to convey meaning in useful ways is key.
Apply	Ability to carry out a procedure	*Foundational*
Analyze	Ability to break problems into constituent parts in useful ways	**Core to Critical Thinking** (rational)
Evaluate	Ability to detect and judge critical, causal factors	**Core to Hypothetical Thinking** (empirical)
Create	Ability to develop a new, optimal solution from a variety of possible scenarios – *note: in Bloom, this level was called "Synthesis"*	**Core to Design Thinking.** This is where the hard work of solution building gets done

FIGURE 29 – Learning Process Dimensions

Key aspects of learning, per Bloom (1956) & Anderson (2001).
Taxonomy in left 2 columns, my analysis in 3rd

Beyond the key learning stages in FIGURE 29, the *Taxonomy* offers an additional view: the characteristics of the type of knowledge gained, defined as knowledge dimensions. These appear in the next table, FIGURE 30. These two tables show the conceptual framework behind what we learn in school. This is what teachers learn so they know how to teach. But to me it's a small step from here to the corporate conference room table, where we struggle with the leader who insists that we're not using critical thinking skills. Again, I see collaboration and learning as being tightly connected, although most of us lack the full perspective as to why.

Collaborators who understand the learning dynamic are better collaborators.

Knowledge Dimensions from Bloom/Anderson Taxonomy		Collaboration Impact
Factual	Low abstraction; specifics reflecting what's observable and thereby *known* within a specific domain (eg., chemistry, economics)	*Foundational – background material, support data*
Conceptual	Includes categories, classifications, and abstract models that define the relationships of problem/solution elements. Important for collaborators as we generate ideas.	**Critical for collaboration.** Used heavily in all analytical aspects of interaction and solution development
Procedural	Understanding how to perform a process to achieve a result	*Foundational*
Meta-Cognitive	Generally *knowledge about knowledge* and the dynamics associated with the learning process	**Essential for advanced collaboration.** Needed to internalize and effectively apply *Collaboration DNA* concepts, especially the ability for a group to shift context in real-time

FIGURE 30 – Knowledge Dimension

What humans know, per Bloom (1956) & Anderson (2001) *Taxonomy* is left 2 columns, my extensions in the 3rd

The stages by which we, as children, acquired these skills are incorporated into the public education system. Most of us have remained completely unaware of all this, though we probably have fond memories of lessons from the playground. Social scientists point to the games we play as children as being primary stages of early, developmental learning[177] which is where we navigated the early levels of Bloom ourselves. We learned to remember rules, and understand their consequences. It was an innocent yet powerful mode of learning. You're it. That's out of bounds. We win. Stepping into the classroom, public education then put us through the paces of the *Taxonomy*. Increasing levels of competence were introduced, achieved and, ideally, retained, as we advanced through grade school, sometimes through higher education, and ultimately, into our adult lives. If we've continued to learn as adults, it's not because someone made us go to school, but because we actually *wanted to* learn. The element of intention in our learning—like intentional collaboration—can be introduced at any stage.

Teachers and many parents know they play a huge role in influencing learning choices and priorities of children. But once out in the workforce we're on our own, and our decisions can come from different places. We might remember and embrace our childhood influences. Or we may make decisions about learning and collaboration on their practical merits, in the moment. Our ability to collaborate suffers significantly if we've missed out on those early, often inspirational learning opportunities. Among the volatile debates around education reform, some have argued that public education has lost sight of these objectives entirely.[178] That means the future-state scenario for collaboration could be more challenging than ever. Here's my take:

> *In every domain of human engagement—*
> *including commercial, social, and public spaces—*
> *our ability to collaborate in the 21st Century*
> *depends on the depth of critical thinking skills*
> *learned in school.*

What does this mean to us as individual collaborators? It means that where we have shortfalls in a specific critical thinking skill, we're going to be less effective. In some cases, that means collaborators will need to go back to basics. To fill our thinking and learning gaps, we must strive to be proficient in all learning aspects covered by Bloom. Fortunately, for adults, it's *not* an all-or-nothing proposition. There's no pass/fail test. There's a seat at the table for anyone wishing to help teams and organizations learn. Recalling Dweck, all of us are capable of continuous learning if our mindset favors growth and discovery, which comes with an element of risk. Collaborators understand and appreciate this better than most. Everyone can add value to the collaborative process in some way if we seek rigor in our thought processes, and we open our minds to what we can learn.[179] We must take some chances, and be willing to be wrong. But the *Taxonomy* provides us with a ready-made roadmap across the learning landscape.

It may be tempting to conclude from Bloom that advanced problem-solving requires only the highest order knowledge and learning capabilities, but each level of competency builds on the previous ones. Understanding this, we can better appreciate the cognitive tools that we must have on our collaborative teams. And we can gain a deeper appreciation of why our teachers tried to teach us the way they did.

It's worth noting that public education is designed so that students traverse and accomplish all of the learning dimensions in the *Taxonomy* before the end of high school. That's good news. With the K12 system under strain this goal can be difficult at times. But if these base skills and learning competencies are established before graduates enter the workforce, collaboration has a chance.

Framing at the Next Level (the Philosophy of Ideas)

Beyond the *Taxonomy*, a long list of analytical frameworks and methods has been built over the centuries to help us define and frame the structure of our new ideas. These too can provide useful inputs to collaboration teams that are seeking to solve difficult problems at advanced levels. The basic idea: navigating competing frameworks helps us understand a bit more about all of them. Better still, we gain the skills needed to create new ones.

Perhaps the best known of these comes down to us from Bacon and Newton as the beloved and famous scientific method. But there's an even deeper history tracing the evolution of how we frame ideas, dating back before Aristotle, Plato and Socrates, all the way to Pythagoras. Their ideas are a rich tapestry, laying the foundation for philosophical and scientific traditions over several millennia.[180] My personal favorites are those developed by Descartes, the Hegelian triad now attributed to Fichte, and of course Immanuel Kant's 1781 Categorical Framework ("CF"). A full assessment of the frameworks mentioned above is best left for another day and perhaps another book.

But FIGURE 31 is a look at some critical thinking in action.

Studying the rows and columns of Kant's celebrated Framework, I saw some new possibilities. In his 3 CF rows I saw epistemologies of rational philosophy (dealing with one archetype), empirical science (dealing with many variables) and real-world complexity (dealing with all factors). In his 4 CF columns I saw a progressive process of problem solving that evolved into FIGURE 31. It seemed to me that relatively dated models can still shed light on our modern problems.[181]

At one level, this is simply some applied critical thinking, a curious mind engaged in a thought exercise, to see what might be discovered. From a different vantage, it provides a useful example of critical thinking across social networks: I developed these ideas on my blog post: "21st Century Kant" and the energy to dig further was fueled from several academics—including a few scientists in Europe—whose interest and energy motivated further study. I might have quickly abandoned the thinking had it been done in a vacuum.

There are always debates on approach and implications, and there are many critical thinking models and guidelines worth exploring.[182] If nothing else, they serve to challenge our thought processes. What I find most fascinating is that critical thinking has pervasive implications that so many tend to leave unexplored.[183]

Critical Thinking: A Notional Framework for collaborating in complex ecosystems		
Step	**Description**	**Rationale and Implications**
1	Define & Scope Problem	**Establish specifics on challenge at hand, in context** - using specific, objective terms; use semantic/narrative frame or simple models
2	Select an Analytical Frame of Reference	**Choose rule system (epistemology) for analysis** – from the following categories: [1] rational, [2] empirical or [3] real-world complexity
3	Explore Choices & Possibilities	**Collaborate** - see FIGURE 21 on how to execute brainstorm process and FIGURE 6 for two modes of discovery
4	Synthesis	**Make conclusions** – document takeaways
from SourcePOV blog post: "21st Century Kant" – see http://bit.ly/povCTk5		

FIGURE 31 – A New Framework for Critical Thinking
From my study of Kant's Categorical Framework (1781);
the 4 rows here correspond to Kant's 4 columns

Did Kant have a working view of complexity in 1781? To me, it's an interesting question. I intend to find out more. I'm hoping that some additional, focused critical thinking—and some research—may shed some light. Few outside of education circles tend to consider carefully what critical thinking means. I'm hoping we can change that, taking intentional steps toward deeper levels of understanding about how we learn.

TAKEAWAYS for "Critical Thinking"

At times I have used the concepts of learning, collaboration, and critical thinking interchangeably throughout the book, though there are nuances in these important concepts. How much of this have you synthesized from these discussions?

- **T1. Can an organization learn? Defend your answer.**

- **T2. Describe a situation where you or your organization solved a difficult problem with critical thinking, where previous attempts had failed due to lack of focus or rigor. What was the catalyst for the breakthrough?**

- **T3. Think of a management team that was successful during your career, in contrast with one that was not. How did each approach problem solving? Compare the prevailing culture of each, and their collective ability to trust. Did they demonstrate a willingness to take risks? To learn? To encourage collaboration?**

- **T4. Define critical thinking in your own words. What makes it important in your career? In your personal life? In setting your long-term goals?**

- **T5. What do you see as the greatest challenge our society faces when it comes to failures in critical thinking?**

These questions and your answers should demonstrate the complex yet powerful interdependencies of the topics we've covered. We're moving now from skills to application. Can you see the possibilities?

21 – An Emerging Lexicon

Pathways to Organizational Learning

I've mentioned complexity almost in passing throughout the book, but its implications have been woven into everything we've covered. The same can be said of *organizational learning*, the broad and somewhat ambitious objectives laid down not so long ago by the likes of Peter Senge, Chris Argyris, and Margaret Wheatley. They have helped us define a broad vision of what organizations must do to reach the next level. Some call it talent development, but I like to think of it as capacity.

In many places I've been planting seeds on how complexity pervades our organizations and influences our interactions. But ultimately, it helps us get at the core dynamics that influence culture, paradigm gridlock and the many challenging organizational dynamics in play. [184]

I developed many of the notions covered in *The DNA of Collaboration* with complexity thinking in mind, including discussions of balance, adaptive governance, flow of insights, and flexible leadership models. I believe any modern-day attempt at organizational learning must recognize these important elements. Ultimately, these factors will serve as critical catalysts. Not that long ago, and certainly for most of recorded civilization, all business happened locally[185] and simplistic economic and social interaction models worked well. In our heavily interconnected world, that's all changed.

We can't collaborate effectively or deeply without applying principles of complexity.

Leaders must understand these factors, because they trump the notions of simple cause-and-effect that much of our conventional business education is founded upon. As I've said, there is much to unlearn ahead. An executive might believe he can change a company culture by simple decree or policy formulation, but the grim reality is that culture is the collective behavior of an organization that is learned over time. It can't be overtly changed by decree. Edgar Schein's perspective on organizational culture highlights this linkage.[186]

Among the many examples of complexity at work in social systems, I think culture is far and away the most important. People seek to fit into their environment. As we study implications of organizational culture, we begin to recognize groups of stakeholders interacting in ways that can lead to identifiable patterns. But for all the benefits of embracing this useful model of behavior, we soon realize the futility of trying to control results directly. But collaborative teams can learn the simple patterns and rules that work in an organization. They can guide changes locally, creating a subculture that allows for desired behavioral patterns to emerge and take hold. In most cases, the best we can hope for is to understand the simple rules for how things tend to work. We can then use this analysis to guide our thinking and potentially influence the influencing forces.

FIGURE 32 on the next page summarizes driving forces and outcomes for organizational culture. Its influence is woven among the threads of our Collaboration DNA, so we should see what else we might uncover. The old cause-and-effect mental model begins to falter under the complexity frame, because the introduction of human elements like free will, learning, and the sharing of knowledge fundamentally change what is possible. In the old engineering model, a system could be defined by the sum of its parts. With complex systems, especially the *adaptive* variety often associated with organizations, it is possible for new outcomes to emerge from the interplay that could *not* have been predicted by a simple roll call of the team.[187]

Social Complexity Example	Organizational Dynamics & Culture
Inherent Properties (known factors)	Principles of Psychology Cognitive Neuroscience (via f-MRI)
What We Can't Predict (unknowns)	What people will do How organizations will behave How a given culture will evolve over time
Frameworks, Models & Paradigms (ways to represent what we observe)	Mental Models Business Models Scientific Method *(cause-and-effect model)* Critical Thinking *(rational model)* Design Thinking *(real-world complexity model)* Game Theory
Influencers (dynamics among stakeholders)	Intention Language & Messaging Trust & Respect in Relationships Engagement Space as Opportunity Adaptive Processes & Governance Balance of Affinity & Diversity

FIGURE 32 – Social Complexity Example
A practical example, made simple (at least in principle)

I believe organizations (and social ecosystems) can learn much from its collaborating teams, allowing the working solutions to surface as *bright spots*.[188] By seeking to replicate the results, organizations can, over time, drive productive levels of change. This is the fundamental objective of double-loop learning envisioned by Chris Argyris a few decades ago, where organizations can learn how to learn and thereby advance their overall capacity to perform.[189]

Complexity has been studied in earnest at the Santa Fe Institute in New Mexico since the mid-1980s. Among those working at the Institute are scientists from fields such as sociology, economics, computer science, biology and physics. Their cross-domain research has introduced new ways to understand systems like the modern organization. They've learned, for example, that control of complex systems is impossible, and that precise outcomes in these spaces defy prediction. Their findings force us to let go of our simple cause-and-effect models in a variety of areas.[190]

Here's how we can tackle organizational challenges using a complexity frame, including what we've learned in *The DNA of Collaboration*:

- **Understanding the concept of emergence—** recognizing the unpredictable interaction among stakeholders (in our case, through group collaboration) as the means for generating new solutions, rather than relying on a structured, highly engineered model for innovation. All collaborative outputs defined in Chapter 3, on Outcomes (including insights, ideas, solution models, and solutions), are examples of creative emergence.

- **Moving away from hierarchy and structure as defining principles—**in favor of flows of knowledge (insight, ideas), leveraging Handy's network model where possible, as discussed in Chapter 10, on Culture. We must identify the ideal amount of structure that lies between imposed hierarchy (top-down influences) and chaos (bottom-up disarray) which is ultimately a discussion of organizational culture, but also a useful way to understand the challenges of knowledge flows in an organization, as discussed in Chapter 19 on Knowledge Management.

- **Shifting focus from control to adaptation—** because we've learned that organizations respond to guidance (through leadership) with performance incentives that motivate in adaptive, incremental ways, rather that strict reward/punishment models that attempt to control behavior. I outlined this in Chapter 15 on Team Dynamics.

- **Understanding self-organization—**in the commercial context, this concept departs from the view of complexity purists a bit, since groups are not "occurring in nature" and thus require some guidance. While complexity sits midway on a continuum from order to chaos, organizational collaboration falls a bit more on the structured side, as we discussed in Chapter 16, on Process.

- **Balance between extremes—**this is an important aspect of understanding the flow of forces influencing outcomes in a complex system, which I outlined in Chapter 17, on Balanced Objectives. The ability of stakeholders to adapt/alter their course of action amplifies the challenge.

Ultimately, complexity thinking is anchored in the practical affairs of the real world. Both philosophy and science are built on models that approximate reality, with assumptions that require simplification and a reduction of variables. Complexity, in my view, is a new type of model that is even more useful than the others because it doesn't require simplification in order to work. The interplay of variables remains intact.

Intentional collaboration changes our approach, opening the door for the first time to tackling complex issues at the ecosystem level. Complexity thinking fundamentally changes how we frame our problems and solutions, but it also informs our approach. The two must work hand in hand.

FIGURE 33 provides an inventory of key concepts that I distilled from *The DNA of Collaboration*. It is both a summary of what we've covered, and a notional lexicon—if not some initial *solution language*—to fuel and inform collaborative efforts going forward.

Solution Language used in *The DNA of Collaboration*				
Problem		**Solution**		
Domains	**Challenges**	**Actions**	**Collaboration DNA**	**Outcomes**
21st Century Team Organization Enterprise Commercial Social Ecosystems ▪ Education ▪ Healthcare ▪ Energy Non-Profit Public Sector	Silo-Thinking Gridlock Barriers Behaviors Structure Hierarchy Confusion Lack of Cooperation Inertia	Empower Engage Foster Demystify Guide Unlock Unwind Unpack Enable Identify Simplify Understand Weave	Models, Frameworks & Paradigms Abstraction Context Focus Intention Language (Semantics) Metaphor Culture Team Dynamics Space (Opportunity) Process/Flow Adaptation	**Insights** **Ideas** **Solution Models** **Solutions** ⎯⎯⎯⎯ Innovations Problem-Solving Learning Critical Thinking Effective Teams Realized Potential (100%) Catalysts Informed Stakeholders

FIGURE 33 – A Lexicon of Intentional Collaboration
Key semantic takeaways from this book

If scale and capital were ultimate harbingers for success in the 20th Century Industrial Economy, the new millennium is exposing different drivers, such as sustainability, resilience, and the construction of stakeholder networks.[191] In this brave new world of 21st Century problem-solving, competitive models may ultimately prove less important than cooperative ones. Organizational learning tips the balance from exploitation to exploration, creating new chances for discovery where before we were obsessed with controlling the gains already achieved. Perhaps this is the fundamental change of thinking that's been needed.

In the 21st Century Knowledge Economy, our models must evolve, seeking a new normal that centers on people—not process, and never technology—because thinking people are the true catalysts for innovation. With focus and energy, we can define and acquire new approaches to influence change within a system—or better stated, within an ecosystem. Intentional collaboration, like organizational culture, is organic—the outcome of humans coming together to make sense of the world, sorting out their relationships in it, and seeking the means by which we might survive, or better still, advance. Smart organizations will foster it and will thrive. I believe that passion and creative energy are lurking inside all of us. Sometimes we're in touch with it, and bring it with us to work. Other times, it's just out of sight, beneath the surface. By now, the subtle power of a good metaphor should be clear.

M24. Ideas are like a Seed.
He *planted* several seeds in the previous seminar.
With *care and feeding*, he hoped a few of the concepts would *germinate.*
His fared best when his ideas weren't *scattered to the wind.*

The notion of a seed's potential can be easily extended to the means of nurturing it:

M25. Collaboration is like Farming.
He *tended his crop* faithfully.
The *harvest* is plentiful, the *laborers* are few.[192]
I plowed into his *fertile* book with energy.[193]
We made sure his ideas had *room to grow.*
The meeting bore the *fruit* of our labors.

Planting and nurturing ideas happens among people every day, whether we realize it or not. Most of the time, we ignore great insights and emerging ideas, and our opportunities for breakthrough thinking are lost to us. Like planting seeds and tending to their growth, intentional collaboration is a designed act, a proactive step to foster creative emergence in our organizations.

For most of the book, I've been addressing the nuances of collaboration on a local scale. But I've also shared how these dynamics shift as the issues gain in scope, scale, and a deeper interconnectedness. That distinction is important as we start learning new models, setting out—with intention—to design our new paradigms. We're still sorting out those details, but defining the broader landscape and the global challenges we're facing are an important first step.[194]

As we enhance our collective ability to learn, we can start to draw roadmaps to new destinations. It's an underlying premise throughout the book, and the theme of Part 5.

Where can we go with our new ideas?

In terms of advancing our collaborative capabilities, you may have noticed I've continued to set the bar high for what is possible. Both the Readiness Framework (Chapter 18) and the exploration of Possibilities (Chapters 19-21) challenge us to change how we think so we can become advocates for change. Many of the new insights and ideas we generate from collaboration can be put to important use. As I said at the outset, our 21st Century world demands intervention.

It would have been easier to stop with process diagrams in Part 4 and declare an incremental victory.

We kept going.

That was by design.

My rationale is that we, as a society—across the world stage and throughout all our social ecosystems—have significant work to do. K12 is only one example. Healthcare is another. Achieving sustainable natural resources is another.

The list goes on. None of these global challenges can be solved by domain experts in isolation. We've tried that. We're going to need to collaborate across domains, and to get there, we're going to need to learn to use all the elements of Collaboration DNA. In our organizations, our schools, and ultimately, all across our world's social systems, there's an overwhelming need for deep, substantive change. We'll need to differentiate which paths make the most sense, and we'll need to make some tough choices.[195]

Early in the book, FIGURE 3 introduced a simple hierarchy of examples to help provide a frame of reference, to provide some context as we built upon the concepts of collaboration block by block. Let's render the same Collaboration DNA concepts a bit differently now, using a wide angle lens for a more generalized view of our relationships to the world and its multitude of interdependent ecosystems.

FIGURE 34 brings focus to the influential role that all of us can play to influence social change.

Global Stakeholder Engagement Models (Where do we want to focus?)				21st Century drivers
World (all-in)				Sustainability Interconnection
Global Community				Global Complexity Value Systems
Commercial Ecosystems (Organizations)	**Social Ecosystems**	**Public Ecosystems**	Covered in this book	Gridlock Shifting Context Social Complexity Culture
Collaborative Teams (8-12 people with intent and a plan)				Messaging Relationships Flow Possibility
Individuals (you, me, all of us)				Abstraction Critical Thinking Focus Intention

FIGURE 34 – Collaborator's Agenda & Key Challenges
A fresh look at social domains where collaboration is required

We can look at this in a variety of contexts, but in short, this diagram shows us how Collaboration DNA can scale. More and more, we're realizing how increasingly connected we truly are, and at some levels, always have been.

Globally, of course, the task ahead seems nearly impossible. Due to the scale of change needed in our world and the powerful grip that culture and old paradigms play in our collective behavior, there's reason to be concerned. But I believe we can change our world from the ground up, inspiring and motivating others from the inside out, one insight and one idea and a few people at a time.

It's got to start somewhere.

Frankly, it needs to start with us.

As I've said before, collaboration is a choice. It's the path we must pursue more often. I believe we can influence our future, and the culture that will guide it. But I believe it all starts with understanding the building blocks of learning.

It starts with Collaboration DNA.

TAKEAWAYS for "Lexicon" and
The DNA of Collaboration

To me, some clear imperatives have started to emerge. These are the takeaways for this chapter, but also for the book:

- **T1. We need a return to intention**
- **T2. We need healthy boundaries and a foundational respect for our colleagues and their contributions (past and future)**
- **T3. We need a bias towards trust, and to be trustworthy ourselves**
- **T4. We need to engage with others, listening in ways we've never listened before**
- **T5. We need more rigor/depth in our thinking**
- **T6. We need to learn how to focus**
- **T7. We need to care**

As you reflect on each of these, evaluate whether they resonate for you in a practical way. Are these approaches to problem solving you are doing today? Or are they approaches you might be willing to do in the right organization?

What would need to change?

In isolation, each item on the list seems possible. That's why I remain optimistic. I've seen profound changes come about when simple changes like these are pursued with a bit of energy. As local teams collaborate more and more effectively on the ground, they begin to get creative on how their ideas might spread. Those local teams gain in scale and influence, and their good ideas spread further still. It's the principle of understanding our bright spots, making unexpected success scalable.

About the Author

For over 25 years, Chris Jones has been driving creative thinking across organizations and project teams, seeking better ways to collaborate. With depth in both leadership and management roles, he seeks to bridge the gap between concept and action, working to make complex theories more accessible. He brings a practical and candid voice to the complex dynamics of 21st Century teams.

Chris is a technology consultant based in Charlotte, NC. He speaks frequently at conferences and has been cited in *CIO Magazine* and *Multisourcing*, a book by Gartner. Active in the social space as @sourcepov, Chris is vocal on the challenges facing adoption of social platforms. He is founder of two Twitter chat communities, #smchat and #ecosys. He is known for being a connector: quick to engage, and always interested in discussing new thinking that could lead to organizational or social breakthroughs.

He attended the University of Virginia in Charlottesville where he received a B.S. in Computer Science. Calling both Virginia and North Carolina home, he travels frequently across the southeast. He is the father of 3, all of them grown. Besides consulting and writing books, his interests include photography, and deeper dives into organizational development, culture change and value systems.

Find him online at http://about.me/sourcepov or on his blog, http://sourcepov.com

Glossary

All definitions provided here are offered in the context of establishing a foundation for effective collaboration. They should be adapted and/or extended as needed to meet the needs of the group.

abstraction—mental thought process that brings different levels of generalization into focus, as a means of comparing alternatives and achieving increased understanding

active listening—ability to be present and focused on the comments of others, suspending judgment and allowing full comprehension of speaker's communication in real time

adaptation—the ability to bring about change (an important type of *emergence*)

affinity—alignment of purpose or intent among a group of stakeholders; important for achieving focus, establishing common purpose, and holding context during discussion; opposite of diversification, serving as a key counter-balancing force

boundaries—arbitrary dividing lines (or *edges*) that defines a space (or *domain*), causing a set of related insights, ideas or broader discussion topics to be grouped together for consideration

bright spots—the analysis of unexpected successes, learning how they happened so we might achieve the same result on a broader scale

collaboration—ability to enhance the exchange of insights and to expand ideas, on demand and in real-time, also defined in practical terms as *solving problems in teams*

complexity—mode of thinking that views the interactions within a system, ecosystem, or problem space (eg., a *domain*) as being highly interdependent and unpredictable, but which can be influenced by simple rules capable of guiding stakeholder decisions and producing fundamentally new (or *emergent*) outcomes

context –a set of related but independent perspectives which we can use to evaluate alternative solutions; our analytical point of view; the lens through which we view a problem

control—limiting actions based on a desire to restrict potential outcomes

critical thinking—an overarching set of mental constructs that influences our ability to collaborate and learn; characterized by rigorous, deep, analytical thinking, yielding careful evaluation of problems in multiple contexts; a useful means for identifying optimal solutions among many alternatives

culture—behavioral norms of a social ecosystem (community, nation, team, organization) that are influenced by the members but not directly controlled by individuals; describes how success is achieved

diversity—the intentional inclusion of stakeholders within a group that possesses broad, differing, but often complementary views, backgrounds, and mindsets, for the purpose of ensuring a holistic perspective; directly correlates with the ability to achieve adaptation and emergence; creates resilience in ecosystems; opposite of affinity, serving as a key counter-balancing force

DNA—the abbreviation for deoxyribonucleic acid, DNA is the set of molecular structures that serve as the genetic building blocks of life; in this book, we're using DNA as a metaphor for the building blocks of collaboration, helping us to unpack the many unique, complex, interdependent attributes that define what is possible in organizations that are seeking to learn and adapt in their environment.

domain—the conceptual space within which collaboration and all aspects of knowledge development occur, made unique by common structural circumstances and dynamics; this book uses *commercial*, *social* and *public* as three primary domain examples, though this specific aggregation can be redefined in ways useful to those requiring necessary distinctions; this includes breaking domains down into sub-domains, often represented by hierarchical diagram (called a *taxonomy*)

ecosystem—the membership and social interactions of interdependent stakeholders within a specific domain

emergence—in the complexity context, the generation of new outcomes based on the unpredictable interaction of a variety of loosely connected agents who interact; in collaboration, this is a key way to describe the original outcomes of the group.

epistemology—(from the Greek: *episteme*) an agreed-upon framework for representing a body of knowledge, including principles, rules, and methods; common examples include science, philosophy and religion, but these may be subdivided to included specific practice domains for sub-specialties within each; *see also "knowledge frameworks"*

factory model—metaphor heavily used in Western culture that models business and education on the structural operation of the factory, with focus on efficiency, cost control, and minimized variation.

framework—a structured conceptual model used to describe something abstract

framing—a stated context for addressing a problem, issue, or challenge

governance—oversight by a group of a given set of activities

hashtag—a Twitter convention for indexing tweets, shown as a character string prefixed with "#" ... important to create Twitter conversation, serving as the basis for Twitter chats; used by communities to organize conversations

heuristic—a predetermined solution used to solve recurring problems

idea—structured thought that is valid in a specific context; can be used to solve a problem

innovation—the emergence of new capabilities in a product or service that drive enhanced value in the marketplace; often positioned by executives as a principal mission of a commercial enterprise; *see also "solutions"*

insight—raw material outcome of collaboration that can also be an input; first notion of a potentially relevant thought

knowledge—the set of all facts, ideas, theories and principles associated with a given domain that describe the collective understanding

knowledge frameworks—the set of rules that govern knowledge within a specific domain; *see also "epistemology"*

knowledge management—a business practice emerging in the 1990's intending to improve the definition, capture, codification and flow of knowledge across an organization

knowledge worker—a person who uses new insight to function in their day to day affairs

leadership—the set of actions, characteristics and skills that inspire others to act

meme—a cultural theme that emerges over time

mental heuristic—a predetermined, learned solution that the human brain uses to solve recurring problems of an urgent nature; this aspect of our neural circuitry is able to trump rational thought in emergency situations

mental models—a personal view of how we believe the world works which influences our decisions and actions

metaphor—a cognitive and literary method to drive understanding that associates an abstract concept with concrete, observable experiences

mindset—the cognitive or emotional bias of an individual, often influenced by culture, professional training, or personal disposition

ontology—a framework that describes the discrete elements that exist within a knowledge domain, including relationships or common interactions among the components

paradigm—a generalized framework that describes the nature and flow of processes within a specific knowledge domain; useful for framing activity within social ecosystems, and as a means to describe qualitative interactions among stakeholders within both problem and solution sets

process—the means by which elements of a knowledge domain achieve an outcome

roles—archetypes for people that perform a specific set of related activities; used in process modeling to define categories of actors who complete specific steps

semantics—the meaning of words in specific contexts, and the basis for using them to communicate

silo—the functional specialty or department within an organization that acts independently of other parts, often competing for limited resources

silo-thinking—the tendency of large, functionally segmented organizations to sub-optimize for the benefit of the function while ignoring the impact to the whole; commonly associated with bureaucracies and cultures that are hierarchical

social—the interaction of stakeholders within an ecosystem

social media—the application of a software-based communication tools and techniques to advance the two-way connection of stakeholders; fostering the two-way exchange of ideas using the Internet; generally speaking, social media is a subset of social technologies, but the terms are often used interchangeably

social technology—the broader set of automated solutions that enable social media and social interaction, including the Internet itself

solution—a productive output of collaboration that addresses one or more problems; if a significant change or improvement, may be classified as an *innovation*, or it may simply represent incremental improvement; *see "innovation"*

solution framework—a conceptual design that defines boundaries, patterns, rules and inputs/outputs for one or more *solutions*; *see "solution"*

space—a time and place set aside that affords the opportunity for creative, intentional collaboration

stakeholders—the members of a social community; an actor in an ecosystem

storytelling—a cognitive and literary method for sharing an experience, as a means to drive learning or foster collaboration

synthesis—the final step in a learning, discovery or collaborative process that consolidates findings, infers meaning, prioritizes outcomes, and ensures retention of work generated

takeaways—summarization of key outcomes

taxonomy—a hierarchical categorization of relationships within a domain

team dynamics—the set of behaviors, responses, and other social factors that influence the potential of a group of people

Twitter chat—social media convention using Twitter that enables a community of stakeholders to self-organize, frame ideas for discussion; a key venue for virtual collaboration; uses a hash tag (agreed upon keyword prefixed with "#") to consolidate group tweets (inputs) into a virtual chat room

venue—a place where collaboration occurs

List of Figures

List of Metaphorical References

References

Ackoff, Russell L., Herbert Addison and Andrew Carey (2010), *Systems Thinking for Curious Managers* London: Triarchy Press.

Albergotti, Dan "The Truth of Imagination: Metaphor's Universe of Possibilities" in *Poets & Writers* January/February 2012. p. 60.

Anderson, Lorin, et al (ed.) (2001), *Taxonomy for Learning, Teaching and Assessing: A Revision of Bloom's Taxonomy of Educational Objectives.* New York. Addison Wesley Longman.

Argyris, Chris (1999), *On Organizational Learning.* Oxford, UK: Blackwell.

Arizona State University (2010, August 19). "Maslow Updated: Reworking of the famous psychological pyramid of needs puts parenting at the top" *Science Daily* (retrieved 5/28/12) http://www.sciencedaily.com/releases/2010/08/100819112118.htm.

Barnes, J. (ed.) (1984), *The Complete Works of Aristotle: The Revised Oxford Translation* (2. Volumes). Princeton, NJ: Princeton University Press.

Barth, Steve (2009). "Koan Zero" (online, retrieved 4/29/12) http://reflexions.typepad.com/reflexions/2009/05/koan-zero.html.

Bingham, Tony and Marcia Conner (2010), *The New Social Learning: A Guide to Transforming Organizations Through Social Media.* San Francisco: Berrett-Koehler.

Bloom, Benjamin, et al (1956), *The Taxonomy of Education Objectives: The Classification of Educational Goals*. New York: David McKay Co.

BMGI: Breakthrough Management Group International (2009), *The Innovator's Toolkit: 50+ Techniques for Predictable and Sustainable Organic Growth* by David Silverstein, Philip Samuel and Neil DeCarlo. New York: John Wiley & Sons.

Bohn, David (1980), *Wholeness and the Implicate Order.* Boston, MA: Routledge.

Brown, Tim (2009), *Change by Design*. New York: HarperCollins.

Buzan, Tony and Barry Buzan (1996), *The Mind Map Book: How to Use Radiant Thinking to Maximize Your Brain's Untapped Potential.* New York: Penguin Group.

Cain, Susan (2012), *Quiet: The Power of Introverts in a World that Can't Stop Talking.* New York: Crown / Random House.

Carlson, Neil R. (2009), *Physiology of Behavior (10th ed.),* Boston: Pearson / Allyn & Bacon.

Chandler, Alfred (1977), *The Visible Hand.* Cambridge: Harvard University Press.

Chesbrough, Henry (2006), *Open Innovation: The New Imperative for Creating and Profiting from Technology.* Cambridge: Harvard Business School Publishing.

Chesbrough, Henry (2008), *Open Innovation: Researching a New Paradigm.* Cambridge: Harvard Business School Publishing.

Christensen, Clayton (1997), *The Innovator's Dilemma*. Cambridge: Harvard Business School Press.

Christensen, Clayton (2008), *Disrupting Class.* New York: McGraw-Hill.

CIBER, Inc., "Getting Smarter, Faster: The Convergence of Knowledge Management and Social Networking" (white paper) by Chris Jones, Goodney Zapp and Gregg Powers (2012).

Dweck, Carol S. (2006), *Mindset.* New York: Ballantine.

Deloitte LLC, by Bill Eggers and John O'Leary (2009), *If We Can Put a Man On the Moon: Getting Big Things Done in Government."* Boston: Harvard Business School Press.

Deloitte LLC, by John Hagel, John Seely-Brown and Lang Davison (2010), *The Power of Pull: How Small Moves, Smartly Made, Can Set Big Things in Motion.* New York: Basic Books / Perseus Book Group.

Drucker, Peter (1988), "The Coming of the New Organization" *Harvard Business Review,* January-February 2008.

Egger, Christine D. (2005), "Wholeness, Understanding and Development: An Episystemic Inquiry" M.A. Thesis 2005, Michigan State University, East Lansing, MI.

Friedman, Thomas (2006), *The World is Flat.* New York: Farrar, Strauss & Giroux.

Gossieaux, Francois and Edward Moran (2010), *The Hyper-Social Organization.* New York: McGraw-Hill.

Goleman, Daniel (1995), *Emotional Intelligence.* New York: Bantam.

Goleman, Daniel (2002), *Primal Leadership.* New York: Bantam.

Goleman, Daniel (2006), *Social Intelligence.* New York: Bantam.

Gray, Dave, et al (2010), *Game Storming: A Playbook for Innovators, Rule Breakers and Change Makers.* Cambridge, MA: O'Reilly Media.

Hagel, John (2010), "Passion versus Obsession." *Edge Perspectives blog* (online, retrieved 5/27/2012), http://edgeperspectives.typepad.com/edge_perspectives/2010/03/passion-versus-obsession.html.

Haidt, Jonathan (2006), *The Happiness Hypothesis: Finding Modern Truth in Ancient Wisdom.* New York: Basic Books.

Handy, Charles (1993), *Understanding Organizations, 4th ed.*
   London: Penguin Group.

Heath, Chip and Dan (2010), *Switch: How to Change Things
   When Change is Hard.* New York: Crown / Random-House.

Herbert, Wray (2010), *On Second Thought.* New York: Crown /
   Random House.

Holley, June (2012), *Network Weaver Handbook,* Athens, OH:
   Network Weaver Publishing.

HSDI: Human Systems Dynamics Institute (2009), by Glenda H.
   Eoyang, *Coping With Chaos: Seven Simple Tools.*
   Circle Pines, MN: Lasumo.

James, Michelle (2012), from conversations with the author on
   flow and structure, Middleburg, VA.

James, William (1890), *Principles of Psychology, Volume 1 of 2.*
   Digireads.com Publishing, 2010 edition, Lawrence, KS.

Johnson, Steven (2010), *Where Do Good Ideas Come From?* New
   York: Riverhead/Penguin.

Jones, Christopher D (2009), "On Cultures of Learning"
   SourcePOV blog (online, retrieved 2/24/12).
   http://sourcepov.com/2009/10/22/learning-culture.

Jones, Christopher D (2011), "The Divergence of Thought in
   Science and Philosophy: Could Complexity be New
   Common Ground" *SourcePOV Blog* (online, retrieved
   2/25/12) http://sourcepov.com/2011/10/31/two-
   roads-diverged-the-great-divide-in-science-and-
   philosophy-can-complexity-be-a-new-common-ground.

Jones, Christopher D (2011), "Philosophy and the Search for
   Ideas: Foundations of Critical Thinking" *SourcePOV blog*
   (online, retrieved 2/25/12)
   http://sourcepov.com/2011/05/21/philosophy-in-
   critical-thinking.

Jones, Christopher D (2012), "21st Century Kant: Learning to Frame Knowledge Anew (with help from Aristotle & Wittgenstein" *SourcePOV blog* (online, retrieved 4/18/12) http://sourcepov.com/2012/01/22/21stc-kant-convergence.

Jones, Christopher D (2012), "KM's Evolution: The 'Connected Organization' and the Emergence of Knowledge Networks" *SourcePOV blog* (online, retrieved 4/14/12) http://sourcepov.com/2012/04/12/km-connected-orgs.

Kant, Immanuel (1781), *The Critique of Pure Reason*, translated and edited by Paul Guyer and Allen W. Wood. Cambridge: Cambridge University Press, 1998.

Kaplan, Saul (2012), *The Business Model Innovation Factory.* Hoboken: John Wiley & Sons.

Kelley, Braden (2010), *Stoking Your Innovation Bonfire.* Hoboken: John Wiley & Sons.

Kelly, Matthew F. (1999), *Rhythm of Life: Living Every Day with Passion and Purpose.* New York: Simon and Schuster.

Kuhn, Thomas (1962), *The Structure of Scientific Revolutions.* Chicago: University of Chicago Press.

Lakoff, George and Mark Johnson (1980), *Metaphors We Live By.* Chicago: University of Chicago Press.

Lewin, Kurt (1947), "Frontiers of Group Dynamics" in *Human Relations*, vol. 1, p. 5-41.

McGilchrist (2011), "The Divided Brain" via *RSA Animate* (online, retrieved 2/26/12) http://www.youtube.com/watch?v=dFs9WO2B8uI.

McAfee, Andrew (2009), *Enterprise 2.0: New Collaborative Tools for your Organization's Toughest Challenges.* Cambridge, MA: Harvard Business School Press.

McKee, Robert (1997), *Story: Substance, Structure, Style and the Principles of Screen writing.* New York: HarperCollins.

Miller, John and Scott Page (2007), *Complex Adaptive Systems* Princeton, NJ: Princeton University Press.

Nations, Mary (2009), conversations with the author on discovery landscapes, including a review of formative models, Raleigh NC.

Nonaka, Ikojiro and Toshihiro Nishiguchi, editors (2001), *Knowledge Emergence: Social, Technical, and Evolutionary Dimensions of Knowledge Creation.* New York: Oxford University Press.

Notter, Jamie and Maddie Grant (2012), *Humanize: How People-centric Organizations Succeed in a Social World.* Indianapolis, IN: Que Publishing.

Noveck, Beth (2008), *Wiki Government.* Washington, DC: Brookings Institution Press.

Noveck, Beth (2012), "Demand a More Open Source Government" via *TED Talks* (online, retrieved 9/15/12) http://www.ted.com/talks/beth_noveck_demand_a_more_open_source_government.html.

Parasuraman, Zeithaml and Berry (1985), "A Conceptual Model of Service Quality and Its Implications for Future Research" *Journal of Marketing*, Vol. 49, pp. 41-50.

Patton, Michael Quinn (1990), *Qualitative Evaluation and Research Methods, 2nd Ed.* Thousand Oaks, CA: SAGE Publications.

Paul, Richard and Linda Elder (2006), *Critical Thinking Tools for Taking Charge of Your Learning and Your Life,* New Jersey: Prentice Hall.

Peat, David (2000), *Blackwinged Night: Creativity in Nature and Mind.* Cambridge, MA: Perseus Publishing.

Pink, Daniel (2006), *A Whole New Mind: Why Right-brainers will Rule the Future.* New York: Penguin/Riverhead.

Pink, Daniel (2009), *Drive: The Surprising Truth About What Motivates Us.* New York: Penguin/Riverhead.

Pluskowski, Boris (2010), "Defining the Social Team." *Complete Innovator blog* (online, retrieved 5/4/12) http://completeinnovator.com/2010/02/09/defining-the-"social-team".

Polanyi, Michael (1958), *Personal Knowledge*. Chicago: University of Chicago Press.

Porter, Michael (1980), *Competitive Strategy.* New York: Free Press / Simon & Schuster.

Rittel, Horst and Melvin Webber (1973), "Dilemmas in a General Theory of Planning" *Policy Sciences*, Vol.4, Amsterdam: Elsevier Scientific Publishing Co.

Robinson, Sir Kenneth (2010), "Changing Education Paradigms" via *RSA Animate* (online, retrieved 4/29/12) http://www.youtube.com/watch?v=zDZFcDGpL4U.

Ryan, Kathleen and Daniel Ostereich (1991), *Driving Fear from the Workplace* San Francisco: Jossey-Bass.

Schein, Edgar (1999), *The Corporate Culture Survival Guide* San Francisco: Jossey-Bass.

Schwartz, Barry (2004), *The Paradox of Choice: Why More is Less.* New York: HarperCollins.

Senge, Peter (1990, 2006), *The Fifth Discipline*. New York: Doubleday.

Sertl, Jennifer and Koby Huberman (2008), *Strategy, Leadership and the Soul* Devon, UK: Triarchy Press.

Siemens, George (2005), "Connectivism: A Learning Theory for the Digital Age," *International Journal of Instructional Technology and Distance Learning*, Vol. 2 No. 1, Jan 2005 (online, retrieved 4/29/2012) http://www.itdl.org/Journal/Jan_05/article01.htm.

Sloane, Paul (ed.) (2011), *A Guide to Open Innovation and Crowdsourcing* London: Kogan Page.

Stewart, Thomas (2001), *The Wealth of Knowledge.* New York: Doubleday.

Tapscott, Dan & Anthony D. Williams (2006), *Wikinomics: How Mass Collaboration Changes Everything.* New York: Penguin.

Tarnas, Richard (1991), *The Passion of the Western Mind: Understanding the Ideas that have Shaped our World View.* New York: Ballantine-Random House.

Turner, Mark (1996), *The Literary Mind: Origins of Thought and Language.* Oxford, UK: Oxford University Press.

Wheatley, Margaret (1996), *A Simpler Way.* San Francisco: Berrett-Koehler.

Wheatley, Margaret (2006), *Leadership and the New Science.* San Francisco: Berrett-Koehler.

Index

Notes

Prologue

[1] David Bohm is an important contributor in the study of thinking, language, and learning in teams; his "leaves on a stream" metaphor was cited by Peter Senge (2006), p. 225. I used the metaphor initially without realizing its source, only to find it highlighted months later in my dog-eared copy of the *Fifth Discipline.* This is an important illustration of the subtle but powerful ways our minds work; sometimes the seeds are planted but we harvest their fruit much later

[2] Wheatley (2006) offers an excellent perspective of our emotional reactions to loss of meaning in the modern world which tends to keeps us "on edge, anxious and sleepless." See her Prologue, pp. x-xi

[3] My thinking has been deeply influenced by several thinkers in Learning Organizations; see Peter Senge (2006), pp. 5-14 for practical application; Chris Argyris (1999), pp. 1-14 for academic and theoretical foundations; and Margaret Wheatley (1996), pp. 56-64 for a refreshing humanistic view

[4] Kanter in *Change Masters* (1980) lays the foundation for understanding complexities of organization culture, bureaucracy and power. Looking back across my own career, I can see how her vision has influenced my approach to solving problems, including elements of corporate entrepreneurship and being an advocate for change; as I turn her pages now, I see much of her thinking has made its way into *The DNA of Collaboration*

[5] Wheatley (1996), p.67

[6] According to Drucker (1988), Stewart (2001) and Tapscott (2006), in no small part due to the Internet, we're pretty much all knowledge workers now. I'll not debate the point here, but in today's world, I think we can all agree how difficult it would be to find someone who isn't actively using new insights to improve their work. See http://en.wikipedia.org/wiki/Knowledge_worker for an expanded view, where I posted some of my early non-original research (per Wikipedia rules!) as a contributor. For a good modern view of *knowledge workers*, see Stewart (2001), p. 9-11, and Tapscott (2006), p. 151-157.

[7] Kanter (1980); as an example of building on her work, I've tapped her notion of working and collaborating *against the grain*, extending her notion of "innovating against the grain," pp. 69-101

[8] Steven Johnson's *Where Good Ideas Come From* (2010) is a valuable source and strong influence on my thinking; see also his excellent TED Talk: "Where Good Ideas Come From" on *YouTube*, http://www.youtube.com/watch?v=NugRZGDbPFU It's worth noting here that, quite often, good ideas come from other good ideas

[9] Jones (2009) "On Cultures of Learning" *SourcePOV blog*, http://sourcepov.com/2009/10/22/learning-culture: note the dialog in the blog comments (with Christian DeNeef, in Europe) that brought Peter Senge onto my radar for the first time

[10] The Twitter communities where I find the deepest insight are: #INNOCHAT (on innovation) #SMCHAT (the possibilities of social media), #ECOSYS (challenges and possibilities in K12 Education), #IDEACHAT (on ideas and creativity) and #BEALEADER (on leadership). Simply use the *hashtag* shown on Twitter to track the latest updates. Links to these communities can be found at http://collaborationdna.com

[11] Thomas Kuhn (1962) developed the concept of *paradigms*, rule systems that frame knowledge in an agreed upon way; he also brought us the *paradigm shift*, a gradual change from one rule system to another. His work is foundational to our understanding of knowledge frameworks. Michael Polanyi (1958) spoke on what we can know in the individual sense, discussing how our observations and judgments filter what we see and what we understand to be true, pp. 18-31. Both men were philosophers of science; both worked to establish a foundation for filters on what we perceive to be true.

[12] My initial exploration on historical divergence of Philosophy and Science and a potential for a modern reconciliation is posted at http://sourcepov.com/2011/10/31/two-roads-diverged-the-great-divide-in-science-and-philosophy-can-complexity-be-a-new-common-ground. My academic grounding in this history is not deep, so I offer this analysis simply to stimulate thinking and discussion. It seemed to work, given the energy in blog comments, almost all of it favorable. I continue to find omissions and the need for changes, and hope that it will continue evolve via virtual collaboration.

[13] See Thomas Friedman, *The World is Flat* (2001)

[14] Eoyang (2009) appears to agree, saying that structured and chaotic models overlap so that "we do not have to choose between them." Prologue, p.x.

[15] Delving deeply into epistemology (or knowledge frameworks) is beyond the scope of this book, but we'll continue to run across some of the challenges associated with differing mental models across the ages. I'll note historic and academic underpinnings where I can. We'll come back to Kant in Chapter 20.

PART A: FRAMING OUR POTENTIAL

01 – Introduction

[16] Kaplan (2012) does a good job describing *capabilities* as a means of defining value in an organization, p.17-29

[17] Margaret Wheatley did not invent the concept of *possibilities* but she may have done the most in recent years to advance our notion of what it means; see *A Simpler Way* (1996), p. 17. I've found a strong intuitive sense of possibilities is a motivational force that can unlock collaboration. It has emerged as a guiding charter for both SMCHAT ("possibilities of social media") and ECOSYS ("challenges and possibilities of K12 Education") Twitter chats

[18] Heisenberg, Werner. *Physics and Beyond: Encounters and Conversations* (1971)

[19] Kaplan (2012), p. 17-39

[20] See Michael Porter (1980) for his classic "Five Forces" model that shows the strategic relationships that include customers, suppliers, competitors, new entrants and substitute products; it's a well-known example of a framework used in business to assess complex market dynamics

[21] Horst Rittel & Melvin Webber (1973) were first to publish an interpretation of *wicked problems*, a class of complex challenges that have been difficult to define, let alone solve, due to interdependency of variables and cross-domain issues, p. 155-169

[22] Kaplan (2012) lends support to the notion of cross-domain focus in our social ecosystems, p.82-84. For a working example of group discussion on change in healthcare and education, see the Med/Ed conversation at #ECOSYS http://bit.ly/ecoeduR5

[23] Aristotle (in both his Nichomachean and Eudemian Ethics; see Barnes (ed.), 1984) is eloquent on the nature of friendship; in the business context there are two primary aspects that come into focus: The utilitarian model, where each person gains benefit from the other; and *teleia philia*, or perfected friendship, where each person acts on behalf of the other, without regard to their own benefit. Most business relationships are the first model which is often sufficient and appropriate. But how much more could be accomplished with the energy and support that derives from the second?

[24] Pink in *Drive* (2011) discusses this, introducing the concept of "a renaissance of self-direction." There is also helpful discussion of the top down approach relative to "bottom up" and "inside out" thinking in the CIBER white paper "Getting Smarter, Faster" (2012), including the table on p.5.

[25] A primary thesis of Notter/Grant in *Humanize* (2009)

[26] Wheatley (1996), p. 36-40.

[27] John Hagel, et al in *Power of Pull* (2010) has become a leading voice in moving from "stocks to flows" and has established a linkage to human passion as a key driver of success in this transition. Michelle James (2012) provides an interesting perspective contrasting structures *void* of flow vs. structures that can *be influenced* by flow; as we'll see later, our mental models should not be taken as mutually exclusive. What is the implication? Today, we are generally mired in presumptions of hierarchy and structure. So while Hagel

speaks to a shift of focus to break the mental paradigm, Michelle James speaks to a generative whole that leverages a balance of extremes. I believe both perspectives are valuable. Either way, we are challenging the premise that structure is a given.

[28] Johnson (2010), p. 20, makes a clear connection between ideas and DNA, exploring the adaptive parallels of nature and culture; in this discussion he "zooms out" to information networks, an approach increasingly used for learning, as evidenced by *personal learning networks* ("PLN"s) that are now popular in public education. In the study of complexity thinking, the notion of a *complex adaptive system* ("CAS") models the adaptive and emergent properties of DNA as well, an interesting area for further discussion; see also Noveck (2012) on collaborative social networks

[29] Wheatley (1996), p. 3: "organizations are living systems … intelligent, creative, adaptive, self-organizing, and meaning-seeking"

[30] Hagel, et al. (2010) extends the metaphor of "pull" on three levels: basic access to resources, attraction of specific resources, and achievement of new things by pulling insights from those resources to solve a problem; the latter scenario is the context I've referenced here. This is all in contrast with "push" as the traditional metaphor of directing what others should do.

02 – Thinking About Thinking

[31] Jones (2011) "Philosophy and the Search for Ideas" *SourcePOV blog* http://sourcepov.com/2009/05/21/philosophy-in-critical-thinking traces the path of my research on critical thinking. While I'm still a student in this fascinating space, several historical inflection points are worth mention. Aristotle is perhaps one of the greatest critical thinkers of antiquity, contributing deeply to concepts that are foundational to modern science and philosophy, advancing notions of taxonomy (categories), ontology (relationships), and four aspects of causality (his "four causes"). Many call Descartes the founder of modern rational philosophy, who brought his knowledge of science and mathematics to bear on those elements of thought that "science" (as we'd call it now) couldn't reach at the time. The final step in his rational thinking methodology is 'synthesis' which is a fundamental process component defined in this book. For more on these great thinkers, see Richard Tarnas (1991) on Aristotle, p.55-68; and on Descartes pp. 276-281.

---

[32] Steven B. Johnson (2010) leads a good analysis of what he calls the *slow hunch*, pp.69-96

[33] I'm foreshadowing Chapter 3 a bit as we discuss the relationship between raw insights and more contextually established ideas

[34] Braden Kelley (2010) discusses the important role of *insights* in the innovation process pp.45-51.

[35] "Inception" a Warner-Brothers cinema release, directed by Christopher Nolan (2010)

[36] Shaw (2002) has had much to say on "messiness" as did Wheatley (1996) and Ackoff (2010)

[37] For an in-depth study of right-brain potential, read Pink, *A Whole New Mind* (2006); see also McGilchrist (2011)

[38] Cognitive neuroscience and the functional MRI ("f-MRI") have produced new evidence on which parts of the brain respond in specific situations. Dan Pink (2006) discusses these concepts from a practical perspective, including in-depth discussion of topics specific to collaboration: story and empathy. Psychologist Ian McGilchrist (2011) provides an excellent update to the discussion of brain physiology, bringing forward and linking together the dynamics of empathy, intuition, pattern matching, and our on-going discovery of context. See also Carlson (2009) for the physiological, text book foundations

[39] Egger (2005), p.29-32, discusses the non-linear role that navigating abstraction plays in our attempts to understand, citing Bohm (1980)

[40] Mind mapping software is increasingly prevalent, built on concept mapping and other visual references that have come down over the years; see Tony Buzan (2000) and several excellent compilations of online resources by Chuck Frey http://innovationtools.com and http://mindmappingsoftwareblog.com; see FIGURE 9 for an example

[41] William James (1890) in *Principles of Psychology, Volume 1*, leads an interesting (and early) discussion of brain function for focus and recognition in Chapter 11, "Attention"

[42] Tim Brown (2009)

[43] BMGI (2009) describes various uses of Ishikawa diagrams, introduced in the 1940's and popularized in the 1960's, to help identify and categorize root cause factors, p. 325-328. A good example of a fishbone diagram used to explain one of our complex problems – organization effectiveness—can be found in Handy (1993), p.15

[44] CIBER (2012) "Getting Smarter, Faster" (a white paper) by Chris Jones, Goodney Zapp and Gregg Powers

[45] Most academic practitioners are content with rules and frameworks that are mutually agreed within their discipline, in part due to the structure of academic tenure, which promotes adherence to the prevailing paradigm (Kuhn, 1962). Kuhn is famous for challenging all of science to beware of paradigm blindness, where the prevailing, over-arching objective may be to confirm what we already think we know. To my (somewhat limited) knowledge, there has been little energy on epistemological convergence to something more basic – such as the pursuit of a common framework – since Kant, in 1781. See also Tarnas (1991) for good historical view

[46] There are many important linkages and implications between effective collaboration and the practice area of innovation. An expanding trend in the space today, closely related to notions we're developing in *The DNA of Collaboration* is called "Open Innovation." This is described by Henry Chesbrough (2006, 2008) and extended into practical applications through a variety of contributors in Paul Sloane (ed.) (2011)

03 – Outcomes

[47] David Gray in *Gamestorming* (2010) talks about divergent exploration and convergent synthesis as part of Game Design (Ch.1), demonstrating a clear parallel between the structure and intent of games and how we analyze problems. After all, learning to play a new game requires problem solving; both have rules, boundaries and desired outcomes. Not only are games a useful metaphor for attacking business problems, games are a good example of an abstract framework

---

48 Many analytical methods exist for the hard work of problem solving, introducing 2x2 grids, visual mind maps, fishbone diagrams and wide variety of approaches to analyzing ideas; a good source is BMGI (2009), *The Innovators Took-kit*

49 Every innovation source in my research emphasizes *ideas* as the primary current of innovation, not *insights*. This may be due to the traditional focus of product R&D, where ideas can number in the thousands. While it is tempting and sometimes useful to link collaboration with innovation, I believe collaboration is more about problem solving, which often results in an innovation. Klaus-Peter Speidel in Sloane (ed.) (2011) makes two key points that reinforce my thinking: (1) "Problem solving doesn't imply innovating. Some problems are solved in innovative ways, but most aren't" (p. 121); and (2) "A typical roadblock for problem solving is lack of information" (p. 121) which is a clear connection to the need for insights. However, there are clear overlaps and synergies that can be gained when studying collaboration and innovation side by side. See helpful discussions on ideas and context by Julian Loren in Sloane (ed.) (2011), pp. 5-14; and the treatment of ideas in the many analytical tools summarized in BMGI (2009). This is also a frequent topic of discussion on Twitter at #INNOCHAT. The ultimate example of an insight in today's world is found on Twitter, in the form of a *tweet*

50 A U.S. News and World Report summary of top charters nationwide is available here: http://www.usnews.com/education/best-high-schools/national-rankings/charter-school-rankings

51 Kuhn (1962), pp. 111-135

52 I sketched out the first draft of this diagram on a napkin one day in late 2009. There is something profoundly inventive about using a napkin as the place for ideas. The napkin diagram went through several iterations before the structure and shape of this book emerged from it. Refer back to this picture often. It's where I first assembled all the Collaboration DNA building blocks in one place. The original, more completion rendition of this model can be downloaded from http://collaborationdna.com

[53] Many of the great thinkers in the field of Organizational Development (or "OD") have expanded on the notion of flow of information and knowledge in organizations, including Senge (1990, 2006), Wheatley (1996), Argyris (1999) and most recently, Eoyang (2009), who speaks to this in the context of feedback loops (Ch.3, p. 41). While Senge expands on Forrester's Systems Thinking model and makes it one of his Five Disciplines for organizational learning, Wheatley focuses primarily on the social and humanistic aspects. Argyris provides perhaps the most intriguing view of organizational capability in his "double loop learning" model, which, at the risk of over-simplifying, introduces a framework for how organizations learn how to learn. Given the iterative nature of learning, the Collaboration Framework in FIGURE 9 clearly reflects the cyclical, "looping back" aspect of flow advanced in various ways by all of these OD thought leaders.

PART B: MESSAGING

04 – Intention

[54] Many motivational speakers and thought leaders weigh in strongly on notions of intention and purpose and how we might reach deeper levels of personal commitment; Matthew F. Kelly (1999) brings a clear voice to a discussion of personal motivation

[55] Wheatley (2006), p. 147

[56] Arizona State University (2010), "Maslow Updated" discusses the latest thinking about the "top" of Maslow's hierarchy of needs

[57] Dweck (2006), p. 6-14

[58] Argyris (1992)

05 – Choosing Our Words

[59] Chris Jones (2011). "Words That Matter: Wittgenstein and Senge on the Power of Language in Critical Thinking." *SourcePOV blog*, http://sourcepov.com/2011/08/16/words-that-matter

[60] Ludwig Wittgenstein was an Austrian Philosophy professor famous for his views on language; ironically his work was very difficult to read. In his primary treatise *Tractatus* (1921), well known for its numbered entries, we find one of his more famous quotes: "5.6: The limits of my language mean the limits of my world"

[61] Wittgenstein (1921); *Tractatus* and his more reflective *Philosophical Investigations* (1953) are considered important 20th century works in the Philosophy of Language and its application

[62] Senge (1990), p. 73; this profound thought can be traced back to Kuhn (on paradigms) and Polanyi (on personal knowledge), and Wittgenstein (on language); our ability to think in new and different ways is often constrained by the words that form our language, and related rule systems that shape (and are shaped by) our cultural norms. In the West, for example, there is a strong bias in science and technology, as reflected in our metaphors, best exemplified by the *Factory Model*, per my metaphor cross reference: M14. David Bohm (1980) points to the subject-verb-object structure of Western language to reinforce our deeply ingrained notion of linear, cause-and-effect thinking

[63] Christensen (2008), pp. 185-186

[64] Aristotle in his *Physics II.9*; *Parts of Animals I-IV*; *Generation of Animals I, II and IV* (see Barnes, 1984)

06 – Metaphor and Common Ground

[65] Aristotle in his *Poetics* (see Barnes, 1984) said "Mastery of metaphor is the greatest thing by far" which speaks to the power metaphors have to bring insight to abstract concepts; he notes further that "a good metaphor implies an intuitive perception of the similarity in dissimilars;" in discussing their intuitive power, Michelle James (2012) noted "you can't argue with a personal, direct experience; it becomes a bridge to the new concept, as opposed to an abstract leap of faith." For more on the power and many applications of metaphor in organizations, see Wheatley (1996), p. 12, and Shaw (2002), p. 122-123

[66] Dan Albergotti (2012) on metaphor in *Poets & Writers*

[67] Lakoff & Johnson (1980)

[68] Alfred Chandler documents the history of the American corporation in *The Visible Hand* (1977), explaining the historical significance of railroads in shaping the first transnational corporations. This aspect of our business heritage has survived in metaphor, buried in the idioms of our language

[69] see Christensen (2008) and Robinson via RSA/Animate (2010)

[70] George Siemens, a paper on Connectivism (2005)

[71] see Johnson (2010) re: metaphor, pp. 3-22

[72] June Holley introduces an excellent guide to social network building in *Network Weavers Guide* (2012), a handbook to guide the purposeful construction of social networks

07 – Storytelling

[73] Turner (1996), speaks from the perspective of a cognitive science professor, at home in the study of human communication via language

[74] McKee (1997), pp. 3-12, is masterful at describing the many dimensions of good stories and narratives, speaking from his vantage as an experienced screen writer and lecturer in the space

[75] Pink (2006) is citing Turner (1996), pp. 4-5

[76] Pink (2006), p. 103

[77] McKee (1997)

[78] Barth, Steve. "Koan Zero" a blog post; (2009) http://reflexions.typepad.com/reflexions/2009/05/koan-zero.html)

PART 3: RELATIONSHIP

08 – Are We Listening?

[79] Kotter (1996) discusses the importance of clear vision that everyone can rally behind, pp.67-83

09 – Hijacked: Heuristics, Instincts and Fear

[80] Goleman (1995), pp. 3-12.

[81] The study of neuroscience has been busy in the last several years getting at what exactly is happening when we follow our instincts. Goleman (1995, 2002, 2006) describes these extremely rapid, almost instantaneous modes of problem solving as "lower brain" or "low road" circuitry in the *amygdala*, not far from regions now known for the functioning of our reflexes and the home of our emotions

[82] The ability to fully prove anything in social sciences like psychology is constrained because of our inability to isolate variables. The human psyche is so intertwined that it's proven impossible (at least, to date) to isolate an instinct, fear, or emotion in order to evaluate cause and effect. This is not to say that social science research is ineffective or not valuable. It's just that the level of certainty is lower, and we remain more reliant on prevailing theories. To a significant extent that is changing, because *fMRI* (or *functional Magnetic Resonance Imaging*) technology is now generating useful data for psychologists. By looking at brain patterns when subjected to a magnetic field, we are able to see which regions of the brain are called upon to work in response to specific stimuli. This is reopening debates about left and right brain function, and also giving us new insight on the topics of Chapter 9.

[83] Peter Senge (1990) discussed this in the context of his *mental models*, with similar concerns about behaviors that resulted in inertia, p. 166-167

[84] McGilchrist (2011)

[85] In his recent book by *On Second Thought* (2010), Wray Herbert explains the nature and subtle influence of mental heuristics. He builds an extensive inventory with numerous examples, behavioral case studies, and some in depth analysis of how our reflexive "quick solution response system" can lead us astray. I selected a subset of examples with the greatest bearing on collaboration, to expose evidence of our tendency to make mental shortcuts

[86] Much of my thinking here is based on original work of Margaret Wheatley; she says: "Darwinistic thought solidified the belief that life was not supposed to happen, that life was an accident, one of many random events. These errors of thought have guide most of our decisions." See also Ryan & Ostereich (1991)

[87] Dweck (2006)

[88] In terms of emergency response, instinct lies in the lower circuitry and is associated more with emotional response (including fear) and, it now seems, mental heuristics; contrast this with intuition, which appears to do much of its work in the right hemisphere, helping us search for relevant patterns from past experience. Both McGilchrist (2011) and Goleman (1995, 2002, 2006) are highly informative on these topics.

[89] ANSWER KEY: Which 3 Heuristics are on a continuum? The following three FIGURE 14 entries operate on a continuum, from negative impact to positive, "quick hit" heuristic to "slow-boat" rational. **[1] Status Quo; [3] Mimicry** and **[6] Simplicity**. Each of these can be good or bad depending on the circumstance. It's difficult to tell if our reaction from the use of these heuristics will help us or hurt us, so the result will be situational.

10 – The Dilemma of Culture

[90] Schein (1999), p.15-26 describes organizational culture as determining "what behaviors will achieve success"

[91] Jones (2010) re: "Culture Change." *SourcePOV blog,* http://bit.ly/povCL

[92] Drucker (2001) in *The Essential Drucker*

[93] Eggers/O'Leary (2009), p.146

[94] Handy in *Understanding Organizations* (1993) establishes an important and fascinating foundation for ongoing discussion of culture in organizations

[95] ANSWER KEY: Sub-Culture Examples

[1] Command: HC – **O/R**; Military - **Joint Chiefs**
[2] Function: HC - **Purchasing**; Military – **Pentagon**
[3] Network: HC – **E/R**; Military – **Intelligence**
[4] Practitioner: HC – **Paramedic**; Military – **SEALs**

[96] McAfee (2009)

[97] Jones (2010) re: Handy in "Trouble w/ Silos." *SourcePOV blog,*
http://bit.ly/povCL2

[98] Kanter (1980)

[99] There is quite a chorus on the topic of silo-thinking as barrier, but
it's worth citing a few of the key voices: Kanter (1980), Senge (1990,
2006), Kotter (1996), McAfee (2009), Eggers/O'Leary (2009),
Notter & Grant (2011), and Kaplan (2012)

[100] Julian Loren in Sloane, Ed. (2011), re: R&D as Silo

[101] Argyris (1999)

[102] Nonaka (2001)

[103] Kotter (1996) is generally authoritative on discrete steps required
for organizational change; his 8-step program is as effective as any
other means I know to frame and pursue broad-scale cultural
challenges

[104] Kotter (1996) re: influence of smaller groups

[105] Sertl (2009) discusses limitations of Command & Control,
introducing an alternative model "Collaborate & Enroll"

11 – Contrarians: On Ego, Power and Control

[106] Wheatley (1996) and Goleman (2006) are both excellent sources
on human desire to be secure, connected, part of a larger whole

[107] The topic of fear in the workplace and its implication is covered
extensively by Kanter (1980), Ryan & Ostereich (1991), and
Argyris (1999). Wheatley (1996) has much to say on this topic as
well

[108] Kanter (1980)

[109] Goleman (2002), p.22

[110] Goleman (2002)

[111] Hagel (2010) discusses passion as a force to overcome
organizational resistance

[112] Goleman (2002, 2006)

12 – The Trusting Organization

[113] Stephen M.R. Covey literally wrote the book on trust in the modern organization. He lays the foundation for his "4 Cores" model in *Speed of Trust* (2006), p.43-123

[114] Christensen (1997) describes examples and factors of "disruption" throughout *The Innovator's Dilemma*

[115] Covey (2006), p.130-132

[116] Parasuraman, Zeithaml and Berry (1985) provided foundational research on the elements of service quality that relate directly to trust. I have used this original research repeatedly in my consulting work with Dr. Eric Threatt, focusing on the value proposition of service organizations, and the key role that trust plays in supplier relationships. Applying the original 1985 framework, we focused on continual improvements in the areas of responsiveness, reliability, tangibles, empathy and trust.

[117] Goleman (2002, 2006)

PART 4: FLOW

13 – Space as Opportunity

[118] Nonaka (2001), Chapter 2

[119] Hagel in *Power of Pull* (2010)

[120] Tim Brown (2009) makes the case strongly for common elements among creativity, design and the emergence of ideas via collaboration; in essence, Brown sees it as the flow of inspiration (emergent insights) across a creative team

[121] Noveck (2012) in a TED Talk on "Open Government"

[122] See http://collaborationdna.com/readers as well as the conversation under Twitter hashtag #cdna, which can be accessed via http://tweetchat.com/room/cdna

[123] Tapscott (2006)

124 Tim Brown (2009)

125 In Sloane (ed.)(2011), p.23, Jeffrey Phillips advocates for smaller teams for the more difficult, "disruptive" agenda owing to higher contact levels necessary to communicate difficult concepts. The larger numbers associated with Open Innovation ("OI") *crowd sourcing*, in contrast, tend to provide a broader sampling of ideas. Both appear to be valuable, but in different circumstances.

126 I've made several references to Twitter Chats that have helped to fuel insights in this book. The first one that caught my eye was #INNOCHAT in April 2009. I founded #SMCHAT that same month, and started #ECOSYS later that fall. All three groups are going strong as of this writing along with hundreds more like them.

127 Conner (2011) re: Social Learning.

128 McAfee (2009) on Google's "20% white space"

14 – Key Roles in Collaboration

129 Wheatley (1996), Goleman (2006) and Senge (2006) are all excellent foundational sources in the social connection among people in organizations. For newer perspectives see Gossieaux/Moran (2010), Conner (2010) and Notter/Grant (2012)

130 Beth Noveck in *Wiki Government* (2009), p.18, agrees on the benefit of intention in defining collaborative roles; she became an early influence on me, moving boundaries on the level of collaboration that may be possible in public places. She helped shape my thinking that spawned #ECOSYS a few months later. Her TED Talk (2012) updated and further advanced this thinking, bringing the concept of *flow* to discussions on Open Government

131 Pluskowski (2010)

132 Many sources here including McAfee (2009), Brown (2009) and Pluskowski (2010); there can be no doubt any longer that *collaboration is a team sport*

133 Pluskowski (2010)

134 Susan Cain (2012) re: Quiet: The Power of Introverts

[135] Pluskowski (2010); for some months in 2009-2010, I had a running debate with my friend and colleague on the value and promise of communities vs. teams. He finally convinced me, as evidenced in my comments on his blog. http://completeinnovator.com/2010/02/09/defining-the-"social-team". Ultimately, I conceded my KM "community of practice" thinking was overshadowing my working knowledge of team dynamics. His post is a great example of public-based virtual collaboration in action

15 – Team Dynamics

[136] In Heath & Heath's *Switch* (2010) "clearing the path" is a key element within their very accessible prescription for driving change

[137] Goleman (1995) says the starting point of empathy is in early childhood; see his timetable discussion, pp. 273-275

[138] Dan Pink (2006) identifies *symphony* as one of the six skills of the right-brain directed future, clearly recognizing its importance in 21st century life; Egger (2005), p. 33-35, also targets the symphony metaphor to discuss *movement* and *pattern*, good examples of how we discern an undivided wholeness, citing Bohm (1980)

[139] Interview with *Pines of Porter* (August, 2012), Nashville, TN

[140] Wheatley (1996), p.67 paints the organization's social landscape with broad strokes, but I come to the same conclusions. She continues "As we look into an organization, we see multiple selves, with messages, goals and behaviors that tell conflicting stories ... the only antidote to the unnerving effects of incoherence in our organizations is integrity" (p.59)

[141] Psychologist Iain McGilchrist ascribes the right-brain with the major role in discerning signals from the environment – especially human signals – that indicate friend/foe, safety/threat – and in the process, align our energies toward an open or closed stance

[142] see also Goleman (1995) Chapter 11; what is worse, because humans tend to adapt to behaviors around them, a closed stance carries the risk of spreading across the entire team. Adding to this, John Hagel in "Passion vs. Obsession" (2010) points out that while "passion builds relationships, obsession inhibits them."

---

[143] Jonathan Haidt a Psychologist at U. Va., in his book *The Happiness Hypothesis* (2006) discusses the importance of overcoming our own natural self-righteousness; with the weight of perceived moral authority, what was previously a simple academic or cognitive advantage escalates into one that's driven and sustained by the emotional passions that morality tends to invoke

[144] See also Kotter (1996) on anchoring to solidify gains

[145] In Sloane (ed.) (2011), pp.7-10, Julian Loren provides supporting detail this view in the context of Open Innovation ("OI") since contributors outside an organization, especially on a broader OI scale, will bring significantly more unique perspectives to the table.

[146] Project managers know the PMI Book of Knowledge well, now in its 4th Ed. www.pmi.org/PMBOK-Guide-and-Standards.aspx

[147] Eoyang (2009) Chapter 2, p. 17

16 – Process

[148] Aristotle in his Physics re: Final Cause (see Barnes (ed.) 1984)

[149] Collaborative Twitter chats include (among many others) #SMCHAT via http://bit.ly/2smchat and #ECOSYS via http://bit.ly/2ecosys

[150] For an example of a long running virtual collaboration using this approach, see the ECOSYS wiki http://bit.ly/ecoedu this group is working to frame possibilities and challenges of K12 Education

[151] When researching critical thinking for this book, I saw the pattern of *synthesis* emerge repeatedly as the final step in the rational philosophy of several philosophers. This can be seen in the work of Descartes *(suspension, segmentation, aggregation, synthesis)*, then Fichte, now considered the source of the Hegelian triad *(thesis, antithesis, synthesis)* and most recently as the final step in education's *Learning Taxonomy:* Bloom (1956) used *synthesis* in the 2nd to last position of the learning hierarchy, but Anderson (2001) moved it to the final position, renaming it *creating*.) Regardless of what we call it, much of the work of critical thinking gets done after the insights are surfaced. I trace the threads of critical thinking on my blog, http://bit.ly/povCTk4

[152] The Open Government Workshop emerged in response to President Obama's 2008 Open Government Directive, with a goal of providing guidance to agencies. The meeting notes for the third Workshop, held in February, 2010, were developed by 4 collaborative teams that included a cross-section of commercial, public at-large, and intra-agency representatives. Team 3 was facilitated by the author, using many of the collaboration practices outlined in this book. Takeaways were posted to a wiki for reference by Federal agencies; as of this writing they were still viewable online:
https://opengovdirective.pbworks.com/w/page/23084024/Team%203%3A%20Feb%2017th%20Workshop

[153] The collaboration forums generating takeaways in this manner included #SMCHAT launched in April 2009 and #ECOSYS, launched the following October. Both communities follow the process outlined here, though ECOSYS, with its focus on long-term social change, follows it more closely

[154] Strong voices on the topic of commercial innovation using social technology include McAfee (2009) and Tapscott (2006). I've advocated *The Connected Organization* as a frame, in hopes it will resonate with executives, Jones (2012) "The Evolution of KM." *SourcePOV blog*, http://bit.ly/povKMv

[155] McAfee (2009)

17 – Balanced Objectives

[156] Wheatley (2006) expands the Journey metaphor beautifully in her Epilogue to *Leadership and the New Science*, pp.189-193

[157] My friend and fellow KM practitioner Kristin Zacheo often used the metaphor of "bumpers" to describe collaborative processes; years after she introduced me to it, the guidance clearly hasn't escaped my thinking

[158] Shaw (2002), p.68-69

[159] Johnson (2010), p.123-128 on designed serendipity and control factors in the R&D context

PART 5 – POSSIBILITIES

18 – Are We Ready?

[160] Kotter (1996) provides good insight on the power of tracking short-term wins, p.122-124

[161] BMGI (2009) provides examples of the radar or "spider web" diagram, p.95-99

19 – The Evolution of Knowledge Management

[162] Stewart (2001) provides numerous examples, p. 130-267

[163] CIBER (2012) "Getting Smarter, Faster: The Convergence of KM and Social Networks"

[164] Nonaka (2001) re: "Knowledge Emergence"

[165] Drucker (1988) "The Coming of the New Organization" appearing in the *Harvard Business Review*

[166] Stewart (2001)

[167] McAfee (2009) Chapter 6 on "Long Hauls" pp.145-172

[168] Hagel, et al in *Power of Pull* (2010) brings focus to the IT business case for improving operational efficiencies, with visibility to the scope and extent of manual exception handling

[169] At the time of this writing, many traditional IT vendors have introduced collaboration solutions that integrate with their core enterprise offerings in useful ways, among them EMC/Documentum, Salesforce.com and Microsoft. Expect more advances in this space. They are critically needed

[170] Hagel, et al (2010) on serendipity, p. 98

[171] Wheatley (1996) and Goleman (2006) re: social desire to connect

[172] Senge (1990), p.270, said "Collaboration is the flip side of KM" which opens the door for either the coin metaphor or the prevailing vehicle for music of the day the 45 record

[173] Jones (2012), "The Evolution of KM." http://bit.ly/povKMv

[174] Kuhn (1962)

20 – Critical Thinking

[175] Senge (1990) re: Personal Mastery

[176] Andersen, et al. (2003) re: updates to *Bloom's Taxonomy of Learning*

[177] Pink (2006) provides a great discussion of the importance of *play* in the 21st Century context, p.185-215

[178] It can be difficult to find objective analysis and research to define the critical thinking gap, given turmoil and debate among education reformers. The fundamental theories of critical thinking can be traced to Jurgen Habermas and the Frankfurt School. Current, more basic conversations focus on requirements for teaching methods of learning and inquiry, similar to the use of *Socratic Questioning*; some basic analysis of K12 challenges and gaps can be found at: http://www.criticalthinking.org/pages/documenting-the-problem/857

[179] ECOSYS wiki http://bit.ly/ecoedu

[180] Jones (2011), "Critical Thinking." http://bit.ly/povCTk4

[181] I find Kant fascinating; especially his Categorical Framework ("C.F."). Specific examples taken from the C.F. itself would include *contingency, causality*, and *possibility,* among a list of 9 others. I explore some interpretations on my blog, "21st Century Kant." http://bit.ly/povCTk5 to see whether we can apply Kant's C.F. to 21st century science, philosophy, and perhaps even complexity. For further input, see analysis of Kant's *Critique of Pure Reason* (1781); see also Tarnas (1991), p.341-347

[182] Approaches to expanding our critical thinking skills can be found in Paul and Elder (2006).

[183] The research for *The DNA of Collaboration* traced on the *SourcePOV blog* included deep dives on culture and critical thinking; true to my message, we never stop learning.

21 – An Emerging Lexicon

[184] Eoyang (2009) provides a very readable introduction to complex systems in the organizational context

[185] Chandler (1977)

[186] Schein (1999) leads an excellent discussion on the nature of organizational culture, p. 13-26, describing its emergent nature, its many levels (both visible and tacit) and the degree to which it exerts control

[187] Miller & Page (2007), pp.93-177

[188] Heath and Heath (2010), pp.27-49, introduce the work of Jerry Sternin, known for using positive deviants to identify successful field results (the favorable long tail of the bell curve distribution) to isolate solutions that are working unexpectedly, to determine why; the Heath brothers opted to use *bright spots* to describe this, on the semantic grounds that it sounded more positive than "deviants", p.272. As an example of practical application, the #ECOSYS community uses this concept to track K12 innovations that work, seeking to identify what would need to happen to allow them to scale in other places; see http://bit.ly/ecoeduB

[189] Argyris (1999) introduces the mechanisms for learning in his double-loop model; these require a change in the governing variables of a rule system, as opposed to merely making adjustments based on undesired consequences (pp.67-91). This discussion is critically important to the cause at hand; Argyris outlines many of the fundamental challenges reflected in *The DNA of Collaboration*, including lack of skills, lack of intention, and the effects of dysfunctional behavior (pp.69-71)

[190] Miller & Page (2007)

[191] Holley (2012), pp.220-260

[192] Matthew 9:37, English Standard Version

[193] John Hagel (4/8/2012), from a Twitter conversation with the author about the *Power of Pull*

[194] From numerous conversations with Mary Nations in Raleigh, NC on the topic of discovery landscapes (2009)

[195] Egger (2005), p.57-58, discusses differentiation and choice as central elements in the process of understanding and sense-making, focusing on the implications for achieving social change

29966031R00166

Made in the USA
San Bernardino, CA
20 March 2019